Restored Gospel

According to

C. S. Lewis

Restored Gospel
According to
C. S. Lewis

Nathan Jensen

ISBN: 1-55517-349-7
v.3

Published by: **Bonneville Books**
Distributed by:
925 North Main, Springville, UT 84663 • 801/489-4084

CFI Publishing and Distribution Since 1986

Cedar Fort, Incorporated
CFI Distribution • CFI Books • Council Press • Bonneville Books

Cover design by Corinne A. Bischoff and Sheila Mortimer
Printed in the United States of America

To Tamara, for her encouragement, support and sacrifice.

And to Mom and Dad, who always encouraged me to write, and taught me that nothing is impossible.

Table of Contents

> And by the power of the
> Holy Ghost ye may know
> the truth of all things.
>
> — Moroni 10:5

CHAPTER 1

The Quest for Truth

Few English writers are as well known and respected as C.S. Lewis. The world has received some of its greatest fiction in *The Chronicles of Narnia* and some of its greatest nonfiction in *Mere Christianity* and *The Abolition of Man*. C.S. Lewis taught at Oxford and Cambridge, spoke to societies throughout Europe, and delivered radio addresses to thousands.

But how is it that this man, a member of the Church of England (and formerly an atheist), a scholar, an author, and a philosopher, came to understand the true gospel of Jesus Christ in such a remarkable manner? This man who, as far as we know, had no substantial contact with The Church of Jesus Christ of Latter-day Saints, and yet has filled his writings with precepts and doctrines that are not only true, but most wholly unique to the restored church.

The world is flooded with literature from Christian scholars who, despite their best efforts, have consistently circumvented the truth and fed thousands with the literary product of their best guess. Still, many of them have done the best they could with what they had to work with. This brings us to the incredible writings of C.S. Lewis. He "hits the nail on the head" in many instances relative to the true gospel as restored by Joseph Smith.

But how? The history of theology has taught us that those who embark on the quest for truth or reality or anything else, without the gift of the Holy Ghost, so often go amiss. Nevertheless, we understand that the Holy Ghost is available to all people — especially seekers of truth. That is what C.S. Lewis was.

"Seek and ye shall find," directed the Lord. This is not simply a book about C.S. Lewis, nor is it a book about his writings in relation to the gospel of Christ. This book is evidence that those of any religion who truly seek high and low for truth will find it — or it will find them. If you are not very familiar with the writings of C.S. Lewis, many things you will read herein will startle you. If you are familiar with his works, no doubt you have already been startled. Either way, I warrant this book will cause you to consider things that you have not before considered.

A word of warning: C.S. Lewis' writings are addictive — his work is hard to put down. He is so simple, eloquent, and down to earth, and he communicates sips of truth so spontaneously, that you get only thirstier as you read.

Sometimes we, as Latter-day Saints, merely accept truth "from the tap." This is our blessing, birthright, and privilege. But, what if we had to "go out to the well" to get our truth. Or, worse still, what if we had to dig our own well, not even knowing where the water was, in search of truth. In other words, we can simply open up the *Doctrine and Covenants*, *The Book of Mormon*, or the *Lectures on Faith* to learn things that have perplexed mankind from the dawn of time. We have only to attend gospel doctrine on Sunday to hear truths repeated that would cause Plato, Kant, and Milton to become dizzy with wonder.

Yes, we turn on the tap, and the truth is there for us — which brings us back to C.S. Lewis. How in the world did he know what he knew? How did he know that it is the destiny of righteous men and women to become gods and goddesses? How did he know pride is "the great universal sin" as taught explicitly by our past prophet Ezra Taft Benson? How did he know that angels do *not* have wings, as believed by most of the Christian world? How did he know that the natural man is an enemy to God and that we must put off the natural man? How did he know about the United Order in a Zion society? And how did C.S. Lewis know that a physical body in the resurrection is necessary to receive a fullness of joy?

These questions go on and on. Until you have read every word that this man has ever written, you will not cease to be amazed at how close — how amazingly close — the ideas of C.S. Lewis are to the truth as we know it. We have modern scripture, Joseph Smith, and all the prophets. What did *he* have? Well, he had the Bible. But so did millions who were clutched with apostasy and who were kept only from the truth because they didn't know where to find it. C.S. Lewis built his basic foundation on the Holy Bible, but only through the Holy Spirit, in my opinion, did he learn truth — line upon line and precept upon precept. No, I'm not proposing that C.S. Lewis was anything akin to a prophet. But, he *was* a humble seeker of truth. Jesus taught that when a man asks for a fish his Father in Heaven will not give him a stone. C.S. Lewis asked for fish and was given fish. The testimony of Jesus is the spirit of prophecy. Perhaps in that sense he *was* a prophet — a prophet to thousands of other Christians not yet ready to look to the "Mormons" for truth, but certainly willing to look to a world-renowned scholar and lovable author. God works in mysterious ways.

C.S. Lewis described himself thus: "I am a very ordinary layman of the Church of England, not especially 'high,' nor especially 'low,' nor especially anything else."[1] Commenting on his own search for truth, he wrote the following:

...I am sure God keeps no one waiting unless He sees that it is good for him to wait. When you do get into your room you will find that the long wait has done you some kind of good which you would not have had otherwise. But you must regard it as waiting, not as camping. You must keep on praying for light: and of course, even in the hall, you must begin trying to obey the rules which are common to the whole house. And above all you must be asking which door is the true one; not which pleases you best by its paint and paneling. In plain language, the question should never be: "Do I like that kind of service?" but "Are these doctrines true: Is holiness here? Does my conscience move me towards this? Is my reluctance to knock at this door due to my pride, or my mere taste, or my personal dislike of this particular door-keeper?

When you have reached your own room, be kind to those who have chosen different doors and to those who are still in the hall. If they are wrong they need your prayers all the more; and if they are your enemies, then you are under orders to pray for them. That is one of the rules common to the whole house.[2]

You will see this kind of direct but gentle attitude again and again. This man seeks for the real stuff, the essence of reality. Although he is not dogmatic nor pushy with it, he is certainly zealous — and oh so likeable. Early in *Mere Christianity* he writes, "I am trying to find out truth."[3] That says a lot about the man — much like Brigham Young who said he would have crawled on his hands and knees to find someone like Moses who could tell him anything about God and Heaven. That was before he met Joseph Smith. Some are content with prevailing theories and notions of the times, whether from science, society or elsewhere. C.S. Lewis was a man like Brigham Young in that this sort of contemporary, cheap knowledge was not enough for him. C.S. looked beyond the transient and the superficial. He looked deeper than where the wind of science happened to be blowing, and as a result made many remarkable discoveries.

"It matters enormously if I alienate anyone from the truth" (*The Problem of Pain*, pg.97), he once wrote. This statement could well be called the theme of C.S. Lewis' life. He has written volumes in the pursuit of persuading people to the truth as well as cutting through propaganda. Concerning this search for reality, David O. McKay, once wrote:

> The world will not admit, nor do we ask it to admit that all these modified views regarding man's place in the universe have been brought about solely by the influence of the Prophet Joseph Smith. God's Spirit is ever ready to guide away from error the sincere seeker after truth; and undoubtedly, hundreds of honest men and women have rejected in their hearts the errors pointed to above without ever having known the truths as revealed to the Prophet. However, the marks of his influence upon religious thought are manifest upon every hand, and whether men acknowledge it or not, the light that came from heaven a century ago is dissipating the darkness that has enthralled the minds of men for ages.[4]

Truly then, the Holy Ghost inspires men of all religions and leads them by the hand, step by step (if they will let Him), to the everlasting Gospel of Jesus Christ. C.S. Lewis frankly admits that his philosophies are not perfect. He once wrote: "I am to give my readers not the best absolutely but the best I have." (*The Problem of Pain*, pg.72) He was very well acquainted with the reality that some people do not *want* truth, especially when it runs up against their pride or prejudices. In one of his well-known works of fiction, *The Magician's Nephew*, he illustrates this truth through fictional analogy thus:

> And the longer and more beautifully the Lion sang the harder Uncle Andrew tried to make himself believe that he could hear nothing but roaring. Now the trouble about trying to make yourself stupider than you really are is that you very often succeed. Uncle Andrew did. He soon did hear nothing but roaring in Aslan's song. Soon he couldn't have heard anything else even if he had wanted to.[5]

One powerful aspect of this relentless quest for truth consisted of finding out what is, regardless of whether it is comforting or easy. He said, "If Christianity is untrue, then no honest man will want to believe it, however helpful it might be; if it is true, every honest man will want to believe it, even if it gives him no help at all."[6]

This idea of people running away from truth, and more especially of inventing a religion for themselves that is more comfortable or less demanding, will be fully dealt with in a later chapter.

C.S. Lewis was also not afraid to venture out a little beyond the straight text found in the Bible. If he felt through logic or inspiration that something was really true, he held to and defended that truth to the best of his ability. He wrote in *Mere Christianity* concerning some of his beliefs that "it is not in the Bible or any of the creeds." (*Mere Christianity*, pg.133)

In order to lay something of a foundation for the rest of this book, it is here necessary to give a brief overview of a few of C.S. Lewis' books — books that comprise part of the essential core of this work. *Mere Christianity* deals with the "common ground" of Christianity as shared by most Christians. It deals with many of the "hard doctrines" of the faith, as well as concepts that C.S. believes are not very well understood in Christendom. *The Problem of Pain* confronts the age-old philosophical debate over why an omnipotent and loving God would allow awful things to happen on Earth. It deals with the harsh realities of life relative to Christianity and examines basic misunderstandings of God and why He sometimes allows us to suffer. *The Screwtape Letters* is a comical, yet insightful, collection of letters from a senior devil to a junior devil giving advice on how to tempt humans. It presents fascinating insights into how the adversary tempts us, and how we react to temptations.

Come with me now into the amazing world of C.S. Lewis and let's look at his fascinating literary contributions from a Latter-day Saint standpoint.

For behold, this is my work and my glory — to bring to pass the immortality and eternal life of man.

— Moses 1:39

CHAPTER 2

My Work and My Glory

One of the great contributions to humanity that came through the Prophet Joseph Smith was the knowledge of the purpose of mortality — and of our potential. That potential, when carried to its ultimate destiny, is to become like God. Knowing that, we begin to see why the Lord takes such an active interest in us, His children. We begin to realize why we must pass through trials and afflictions, persecutions, and wrongdoing, and eventually die. It is because our Lord is trying to take our raw material and make us into something glorious — something capable of eternal life and exaltation. Heaven is not like a toy that can just be given to us; it is something we must be thoroughly prepared for. It must be inside us before we can be inside it. That is why the Lord chastens us. He chastens because he loves us. He is trying to refine us like gold and turn us into new creatures — if we will only let Him. C.S. Lewis had a striking understanding of all of this. He somehow knew our purpose and knew why God works with us so. Consider the following writing of C.S. Lewis:

He wanted to make Saints; gods; things like Himself...(*The Screwtape Letters*, pg.120) But if you are a poor creature — poisoned by a wretched upbringing in some house full of vulgar jealousies and senseless quarrels — saddled, by no choice of your own, with some loathsome sexual perversion — nagged day in and day out by an inferiority complex that makes you snap at your best friends — do not despair. He knows all about it. You are one of the poor whom He blessed. He knows what a wretched machine you are trying to drive. Keep on. Do what you can. One day (perhaps in another world, but perhaps far sooner than that) he will fling it on the scrap-heap and give you a new one. And then you may astonish us all — not least yourself: for you have learned your driving in a hard school. That is why He warned people to "count the cost" before becoming Christians. "Make no mistake," He says, "if you let me, I will make you perfect. The moment you put yourself in My hands, that is what you are in for. Nothing less, or other, than that. You have free will, and if you choose, you can push Me away. But if you do not push Me away, understand that I am going to see this job through. Whatever suffering it may cost you in your earthly life, whatever inconceivable purification it may cost you after death, whatever it costs Me, I will never rest, nor let you rest, until you are literally perfect — until my Father can say without reservation that He is well pleased with you, as He said He was well pleased with me. This I can do and will do. But I will not do anything less.

And yet — this is the other and equally important side of it — this Helper who will, in the long run, be satisfied with nothing less than absolute perfection, will also be delighted with the first feeble, stumbling effort you make tomorrow to do the simplest duty. [7]

What a marvelous comprehension he had! He knew that God has sent us down here to a "hard" school for a reason. Why does it have to be so hard? The lessons in life that stick with you the longest are those that have been learned "the hard way." He wants us to really learn. And when we have learned we must grow. And when we have grown then we are in the process of coming back to Him. The stakes are so high down here. Satan is fighting tooth and nail for our souls as well as God. Will we choose happiness or misery? Satan would force us to him if he could, but God will not force us. However, He will do everything in his power to show us that it is only through Him that we can be happy forever. But, He doesn't have much time to work with us. That is why this life is like boot camp — sort of a crash course, with lots of mistakes, successes and hard learning along the way. One fact that makes it all so crucial is that our Heavenly Father cannot look upon sin with the least degree of allowance.[8] He said so Himself to the prophet Joseph Smith. C.S. Lewis understood this, also. He wrote:

To ask that God's love should be content with us as we are is to ask that God should cease to be God: because He is what He is, His love must, in the nature of things, be impeded and repelled by certain stains in our present character, and because He already loves us He must labour to make us lovable. We cannot even wish, in our better moments, that He could reconcile Himself to our present impurities — no more than the beggar maid could wish that King Cophetua should be content with her rags and dirt, or a dog, once having learned to love man, could wish that man were such as to tolerate in his house the snapping, verminous, polluting creature of the wild pack. What we would here and now call our "happiness" is not the end God chiefly has in view: but when we are such as He can love without impediment, we shall in fact by happy.[9]

This metamorphosis God is trying to put us through hurts, but it is for our own good. Neal A. Maxwell spoke of this doctrine in the following way:

> So much depends, therefore, upon our maintaining gospel perspective in the midst of ordinariness, the pressures of tempta- tion, tribulation, deprivation, and the cares of the world. As we come to love the Lord more and more, we can understand rather than resent His purposes. Besides, He who should know has said "there is no other way." Furthermore, since there is but one path back to our true home, this wisdom by C.S. Lewis is worth pondering: "Our Father in Heaven refreshes us on the journey through life with some pleasant inns, but he will not encourage us to mistake them for home."[10]

C.S. Lewis said:

> [The Christian doctrine of suffering explains, I believe, a very curious fact about the world we live in. The settled happiness and security which we all desire, God withholds from us by the very nature of the world: but joy, pleasure, and merriment He has scat- tered broadcast. We are never safe, but we have plenty of fun, and some ecstasy. It is not hard to see why. The security we crave would teach us to rest our heart in this world and oppose an obstacle to our return to God: a few moments of happy love, a landscape, a symphony, a merry meeting with our friends, a bathe or a football match, have no such tendency. Our Father refreshes us on the journey with some pleasant inns, but will not encourage us to mistake them for home.[11]]

Perhaps some resent the fact that [God rarely lets us become too comfortable on this old Earth. Every time we start to get really cozy in the world, something seems to come along that turns our whole world upside down and makes us search for something deeper than our cars or vacations. On the surface, most of us want to become completely comfortable in the world. We want security and money and cars and houses. But this state of mind is disas- trous for our eternal well-being. How can we embrace a celestial world when we have already become inseparably connected with our present telestial world? Jesus told the young rich man to sell everything he had and give it all to the poor, and to come and follow Him.] He asks us to forsake the world, to flee Babylon. "But," we ask, "why can't He just let us enjoy this life to the fullest?" The reason, I think, is because, metaphorically speaking, all we're doing here is making mud pies. We want to be left alone in our pleasures of grovelling in the mud. But there is so much more in store for us, and thus the necessity of our painful remaking. C.S. Lewis has said:

> Everyone has noticed how hard it is to turn our thoughts to God when everything is going well with us. We "have all we want" is a terrible saying when "all" does not include God. We find God an interruption...We regard God as an airman regards his parachute; it's there for emergencies but he hopes he'll never have to use it. (*The Problem of Pain*, pg.96)

The Book of Mormon verifies this. In Alma 46:8 we are taught the following truth: "Thus we see how quick the children of men do forget the Lord their God, yea, how quick to do iniquity, and to be led away by the evil one." In Deuteronomy 4:30 we read, "When thou art in tribulation, and all these things are come upon thee, [even] in the latter days, if thou turn to the LORD thy God, and shalt be obedient unto his voice..." C.S. Lewis expounds further:

> Now God, who has made us, knows what we are and that our happiness lies in Him. Yet we will not seek it in Him as long as He leaves us any other resort where it can even plausibly be looked for. While what we call "our own life" remains agreeable we will not surrender it to Him. What then can God do in our interest but make "our own life" less agreeable to us, and take away the plausible sources of false happiness?[12]

After Job's terrible affliction he was no doubt stronger, happier, and much more fit for eternal life. The glory of exaltation cannot be born by the wicked, the weak, the soft, or the indulgent. This is something for heroes — men and women of God. The Lord revealed the following to the Prophet Joseph Smith:

> For verily I say unto you, blessed is he that keepeth my commandments, whether in life or in death; and he that is faithful in tribulation, the reward of the same is greater in the kingdom of heaven.[13]

The reward is greater for those who endure tribulation well! For the bumps and bruises that God allows us right now we will someday thank Him. For the persecutions we endure for the sake of Christ we will someday rejoice to have had the privilege of sharing in. Paul of old rejoiced in tribulation. He knew that his was a celestial soul in the making. What a grand perspective! In D&C 58:4 we read, "For after much tribulation come the blessings. Wherefore the day cometh that ye shall be crowned with much glory; the hour is not yet, but is nigh at hand." Bruce R. McConkie expounded on this concept in the following way:

"Tribulation worketh patience" (Rom. 5:3; 12:12; D&C 54:10), and it is only "through much tribulation" that men may "enter into the kingdom of God." (Acts 14:22) "He that is faithful in tribulation, the reward of the same is greater in the kingdom of heaven. Ye cannot behold with your natural eyes, for the present time, the design of your God concerning those things which shall come hereafter, and the glory which shall follow after much tribulation. For after much tribulation come the blessings." (D&C 58:2-4; 103:12) Exalted beings are described in these words: "These are they which came out of great tribulation, and have washed their robes, and made them white in the blood of the Lamb." (Rev. 7:14) The saints glory in tribulation. (Rom. 5:3; D&C 127:2)[14]

The Lord Himself explained His "tough love," and all the chastening and refining as follows:

Behold, the great day of the Lord is at hand; and who can abide the day of his coming, and who can stand when he appeareth? For he is like a refiner's fire, and like fuller's soap; and he shall sit as a refiner and purifier of silver, and he shall purify the sons of Levi, and purge them as gold and silver, that they may offer unto the Lord an offering in righteousness.[15]

Compare these ideas with those of C.S. Lewis:

[I am not arguing that pain is not painful. Pain hurts. That is what the word means. I am only trying to show that the old Christian doctrine of being made "perfect through suffering" is not incredible.] To prove it palatable is beyond my design.[16]

Which of us can welcome suffering because we know it will make us better and stronger? But the doctrine is true and we must square ourselves with this truth. The Lord lets us suffer sometimes because He loves us, not because He does not care about us. Here is more evidence as to how the Lord gets our attention and uses "bad" means for "good" ends. In a revelation to Joseph Smith, the Lord said:

How oft have I called upon you by the mouth of my servants, and by the ministering of angels, and by mine own voice, and by the voice of thunderings, and by the voice of lightnings, and by the voice of tempests, and by the voice of earthquakes, and great hailstorms, and by the voice of famines and pestilences of every kind, and by the great sound of a trump, and by the voice of judgment, and by the voice of mercy all the day long, and by the voice of glory and honor and the riches of eternal life, and would have saved you with an everlasting salvation, but ye would not!¹⁷

It is unfortunate that our hard-heartedness necessitates the use of such unpleasantries in order to jerk us back to reality — the reality of why we are here and what the Lord is trying so benevolently to do for us. Bruce R. McConkie throws some light on the whole concept. He wrote about what we must do to cast off our old self and become a true and final convert to God's way. He wrote:

A convert is one who has put off the natural man, yielded to the enticings of the Holy Spirit, and become "a saint through the atonement of Christ the Lord." Such a person has become "as a child, submissive, meek, humble, patient, full of love, willing to submit to all things which the Lord seeth fit to inflict upon him, even as a child doth submit to his father." (Mosiah 3:19) He has become a new creature of the Holy Ghost: the old creature has been converted or changed into a new one. He has been born again: where once he was spiritually dead, he has been regenerated to a state of spiritual life. (Mosiah 27:24-29) In real conversion, which is essential to salvation (Matt. 18:3), the convert not only changes his beliefs, casting off the false traditions of the past and accepting the beauties of revealed religion, but he changes his whole way of life, and the nature and structure of his very being is quickened and changed by the power of the Holy Ghost.¹⁸

As he said, we must cast off all of the old traditions, beliefs, and habits that are not consistent with the gospel of Jesus Christ. Or, put another way, we must inevitably kill that part of us which is not consistent with joy. We are to, as Elder Neal A. Maxwell once said, lay the animal within us upon the alter to be consumed. We can't slouch and compromise our way into everlasting joy. We must cast off the natural man and embrace the Holy Spirit. But that is very hard. In fact, it is virtually impossible while we are in the midst of enjoying worldliness, prosperity, and indulgence. That is why God is continually trying to wake us up out of our stagnant slumber. C.S. Lewis compares what God is trying to do with us to a sculptor's shop. He said:

And that is precisely what Christianity is about. This world is a great sculptor's shop. We are the statues and there is a rumour going round the shop that some of us are some day going to come to life.[19]

Ezra Taft Benson referred to it as "living more abundantly." He said:

> The gospel of Jesus Christ has always been essentially a plan for living more abundantly. To do so requires righteous, worthwhile effort and application. If we are to pattern our lives in accordance with the divine example set for us by the Savior, we must attain to that stature by releasing and developing our capacities to the fullest through devoted service. Only in this way may we become worthy examples of the kingdom of God on earth and merit consideration for membership in the kingdom of God in heaven.[20]

C.S. Lewis offers another interesting commentary on how God works with us and what He is about. He wrote:

> The Christian way is different: harder, and easier. Christ says "Give me All. I don't want so much of your time and so much of your money and so much of your work: I want You. I have not come to torment your natural self, but to kill it. No half-measures are any good. I don't want to cut off a branch here and a branch there, I want to have the whole tree down. I don't want to drill the tooth, or crown it, or stop it, but to have it out. Hand over the whole natural self, all the desires which you think innocent as well as the ones you think wicked — the whole outfit. I will give you a new self instead. In fact, I will give you Myself: my own will shall become yours.[21]

One great example of the process is how Jehovah dealt with the children of Israel in the wilderness. The entire story is one great symbol after another of how God works with individual lives. First, God delivered the children of Israel from Egyptian bondage just as He can deliver us from sin. Then, He tried to give them eternal laws that would make them forever happy. When they rejected this law, He did not outrightly reject them, but he could not indulge them, either. He gave them a lower law and had them wander and suffer in the wilderness for 40 years before they could enter the promised land. When we sin or turn away from God, He usually gives us our own hand-tailored "wilderness." This gives us the opportunity to suffer a little and get a few things straight. Afterwards, if we're faithful, there will be the promised land waiting for us. But, before that time comes, He is going to try to make us perfect. C.S. Lewis wrote:

The command *Be ye perfect* is not idealistic gas. Nor is it a command to do the impossible. He is going to make us into creatures that can obey that command. He said (in the Bible) that we're "gods" and He is going to make good His words. If we let Him — for we can prevent Him, if we choose — He will make the feeblest and filthiest of us into a god or goddess, a dazzling, radiant, immortal creature, pulsating all through with such energy and joy and wisdom and love as we cannot now imagine, a bright stainless mirror which reflects back to God perfectly (though, of course, on a smaller scale) His own boundless power and delight and goodness. The process will be long and in parts very painful; but that is what we are in for. Nothing less. He meant what He said.[22]

God's work and His glory is to bring about our immortality and eternal life. That is no little feat. It is like turning a crawling, slithering little worm of a thing (a caterpillar) that gropes around in the dirt into a beautiful, delicate creature that explodes off of the ground and flies around in the heavens (a butterfly). C.S. Lewis somehow knew what was taught in Moses 1:39 when he wrote, "The glory of God, and, as our only means to glorifying Him, the salvation of human souls, is the real business of life."[23] He also believed that God tries to mold us so, because He loves us so. He wrote:

Here is another way of putting the two sides of the truth. On the one hand we must never imagine that our own unaided efforts can be relied on to carry us even through the next twenty-four hours as "decent" people. If He does not support us, not one of us is safe from some gross sin. On the other hand, no possible degree of holiness or heroism which has ever been recorded of the greatest saints is beyond what He is determined to produce in every one of us in the end. The job will not be completed in this life: but He means to get us as far as possible before death. We are, not metaphorically but in very truth, a Divine work of art, something that God is making, and therefore something with which He will not be satisfied until it has a certain character. Here again we come up against what I have called the 'intolerable compliment'. Over a sketch made idly to amuse a child, an artist may not take much trouble: he may be content to let it go even though it is not exactly as he meant it to be. But over the great picture of his life — the work which he loves, though in a different fashion, as intensely as a man loves a woman or a mother a child — he will take endless trouble — and would, doubtless, thereby give endless trouble to the picture if it were sentient. One can imagine a sentient picture, after being rubbed and scraped and re-commenced for the tenth time, wishing that it were only a thumb-nail sketch whose making was over in a minute. In the same way, it is natural for us to wish that God had designed for us a less glorious and less arduous destiny; but then we are wishing not for more love but for less.[24]

C.S. Lewis calls it the "intolerable compliment" — the strange fact that God should love us so much. If He didn't, why should He bother with us? If He demands so much of us (which He certainly does — Jesus told us to be perfect like He is) then certainly no religion that says, "Do whatever you please, and you'll still be saved," can possibly be the true religion, or the religion God intends for us. When God called Joseph Smith to usher in the dispensation of the fullness of times, He also asked a great deal of those who would become a part of this great dispensation. Joseph taught the following to the School of the Prophets in Kirtland:

> Let us here observe, that a religion that does not require the sacrifice of all things never has power sufficient to produce the faith necessary unto life and salvation; for, from the first existence of man, the faith necessary unto the enjoyment of life and salvation never could be obtained without the sacrifice of all earthly things. It was through this sacrifice, and this only, that God has ordained that men should enjoy eternal life; and it is through the medium of the sacrifice of all earthly things that men do actually know that they are doing the things that are well pleasing in the sight of God. When a man has offered in sacrifice all that he has for the truth's sake, not even withholding his life, and believing before God that he has been called to make this sacrifice because he seeks to do his will, he does know, most assuredly, that God does and will accept his sacrifice and offering, and that he has not, nor will not seek his face in vain. Under these circumstances, then, he can obtain the faith necessary for him to lay hold on eternal life.[25]

This "sacrifice of all things" seems a hard request. But God also said that our afflictions would be only "a small moment," and that if we endured it well we would be exalted. When you look at the big picture, God requires very little at our hands compared with what He will bless us with for eternity if we are faithful. But it is very difficult to "fight the good fight" and work and struggle to align ourselves with God when we feel self-sufficient or very comfortable and at ease in the world. The prophets have told us such time and again, and *The Book of Mormon* makes it very clear, even repetitively clear. C.S. Lewis understood the principle. He wrote:

This illusion of self-sufficiency may be at its strongest in some very honest, kindly, and temperate people, and on such people, therefore, misfortune must fall. The dangers of apparent self-sufficiency explain why Our Lord regards the vices of the feckless and dissipated so much more leniently than the vices that lead to worldly success. Prostitutes are in no danger of finding their present life so satisfactory that they cannot turn to God: the proud, the avaricious, the self-righteous, are in that danger. (*The Problem of Pain*, pg.98)

We well remember President Ezra Taft Benson's earth-shaking talk on pride, and how the rich and the learned are particularly susceptible to this subtle evil. When pride creeps in, we tend to push the Lord out of our lives. And now, one last excerpt from our Oxford scholar who seemed to understand much of the plan of salvation so well:

The real Son of God is at your side. He is beginning to turn you into the same kind of thing as Himself. He is beginning, so to speak, to "inject" His kind of life and thought, His *Zoe*, into you; beginning to turn the tin soldier into a live man. The part of you that does not live is the part that is still tin.

We may be content to remain what we call "ordinary people:" but He is determined to carry out a quite different plan. To shrink back from that plan is not humility; it is laziness and cowardice. To submit to it is not conceit or megalomania; it is obedience.[26]

The "tin soldier" is an effective analogy. While we yet remain like the natural man, we are really not yet fully alive. Our life is largely shaped by nature and the forces around us like an ocean wave carries a bottle. We have a body and attributes like God mainly in toy-like fashion. But when we cast off the natural man, we become fully real, fully alive, and as capable of joy as our Heavenly Father.

"Be ye therefore perfect,
even as your Father which
is in heaven is perfect."

— Matthew 5:48

CHAPTER 3

Perfecting Ourselves

Eternal progression is one of the cornerstones of the restored gospel. We know that as a church and as individuals we are to take very seriously the command of Christ to be perfect. We are gods and goddesses in the making and our Heavenly Father will, ultimately, demand nothing less than perfection; for He cannot look upon sin with the least degree of allowance. We also understand, however, that God is very patient with us along the path. We often make mistakes, stumble, get off the path, and sometimes even turn around and walk the opposite way. That is why repentance is so crucial. The Lord expects us to continue to repent, to work out our own salvations with fear and trembling, and to seek to perfect ourselves. C.S. Lewis seemed to be well acquainted with this principle. He once said:

I find a good many people have been bothered by what I said in the last chapter about Our Lord's words, "Be ye perfect." Some people seem to think this means "Unless you are perfect, I will not help you;" and as we cannot be perfect, then, if He meant that, our position is hopeless. But I do not think He did mean that. I think He meant "The only help I will give is help to become perfect. You may want something less: but I will give you nothing less."[27]

God told Moses that His work and glory was to bring about the eternal life of man.[28] This is serious business. It is a grand and horrendous effort for each one of us, and the Lord is committed to do all that He can. The rest depends upon us — upon our agency. The vital element in all of this is sincere repentance and a turning away from our evil ways. Elder Bruce R. McConkie noted the following:

To gain forgiveness through repentance a person must have a conviction of guilt, a godly sorrow for sin, and a contrite spirit. He must desire to be relieved of the burden of sin, have a fixed determination to forsake his evil ways, be willing to confess his sins, and forgive those who have trespassed against him; he must accept the cleansing power of the blood of Christ as such is offered through the waters of baptism and the conferral of the Holy Ghost.[29]

C.S. Lewis understood that it is only through the atoning blood of Christ that we can be saved. He also had another perspective on repentance in regards to the amount of time that passes after a sin is committed. If a lot of time passes after an unrepented sin, does that sin just sort of fade away, along with our memory of the sin? This is something that perhaps many have wondered about. Consider the following view of C.S. Lewis:

> We have a strange illusion that mere time cancels sin. I have heard others, and I have heard myself, recounting cruelties and falsehoods committed in boyhood as if they were no concern of the present speaker's, and even with laughter. But mere time does nothing either to the fact or to the guilt of a sin. The guilt is washed out not by time but by repentance and the blood of Christ.[30]

This view is probably substantiated by not only common sense, but by the doctrine of past sins returning when we sin, repent, and then later commit the same sin again. Regardless, the most important factor is that of how our sins are washed away: through the atoning sacrifice of the Lord.

Now let us divert our attention for a moment to the law of Moses. This has seemed like a very strict law, and perhaps a legalistic system. One in which people had to live within very specific boundaries all the time. Of course, the law of Christ, or the fullness of the gospel, is based more around the spirit of the law than the letter of the law. Ultimately, it is no less strict. In *The Book of Mormon* we read of this:

> And now I say unto you that it was expedient that there should be a law given to the children of Israel, yea, even a very strict law; for they were a stiffnecked people, quick to do iniquity, and slow to remember the Lord their God;[31]

C.S. Lewis comments on the law of Christ, and part of the purpose behind it. He wrote, "We might think that God wanted simply obedience to a set of rules; whereas He really wants people of a particular sort." (*Mere Christianity*, pg.63) God isn't as concerned about every particular of our lives — of what we have or have not done at any given moment in our life — as He is about our becoming the kind of soul that He wants us to be. The kind of soul that is wholly righteous, not just in an outward sort of way, but permeating deeply into the very fiber of our character and destiny. In order to attain this state, we must ultimately be completely clean and free of sin. Spencer W. Kimball commented on the principle in this way:

> The reason is forthrightly stated by Nephi — "...There cannot any unclean thing enter into the Kingdom of God..." (1 Ne. 15:34) And again, "...no unclean thing can dwell with God..." (1 Ne. 10:21) To the prophets the term unclean in this context means what it means to God. To man the word may be relative in meaning — one minute speck of dirt does not make a white shirt or dress unclean, for example. But to God who is perfection, cleanliness means moral and personal cleanliness. Less than that is, in one degree or another, uncleanliness and hence cannot dwell with God.[32]

C.S. Lewis understood that even though our goal is perfection, we are not now perfect. That is why God has given us a lifetime to repent and try to become more like God. However, he also understood that we must never give up our quest for perfection, no matter how slow, at times, we seem to be moving in the right direction. He said, "The only fatal thing is to sit down content with anything less than perfection." (*Mere Christianity*, pg.79) The reason this is so crucial for our long-term joy is that joy is inseparably linked to goodness. If we become filthy creatures, then joy will repulse us and we it. We will cleave to those things that are most like us. It happens here on Earth and it will happen in the next life. The *Doctrine and Covenants* offers an inspired perspective on this principle. It reads:

> For intelligence cleaveth unto intelligence; wisdom receiveth wisdom; truth embraceth truth; virtue loveth virtue; light cleaveth unto light; mercy hath compassion on mercy and claimeth her own; justice continueth its course and claimeth its own; judgment goeth before the face of him who sitteth upon the throne and governeth and executeth all things.[33]

Because of Joseph Smith, we as Latter-day Saints understand that things of the earth often hint about the things of heaven, and beauty here is similar to beauty there. Joseph taught:

> Every honest man who has visited the city of Nauvoo since it existed, can bear record of better things, and place me in the front ranks of those who are known to do good for the sake of good-

ness, and show all liars, hypocrites and abominable creatures that, while vice sinks them down to darkness and woe, virtue exalts me and the Saints to light and immortality.[34]

Recall the teaching of Ezra Taft Benson in which he said that the Lord's ways are different from those of the world. He said:

> The Lord works from the inside out. The world works from the outside in. The world would take people out of the slums. Christ takes the slums out of people, and then they take themselves out of the slums. The world would mold men by changing their environment. Christ changes men, who then change their environment. The world would shape human behavior, but Christ can change human nature.[35]

Thus we see that personal purity is essential in our quest for perfection. Being perfect like the Savior does not come through advanced education, heightened intellect, enlightened society, or super science; it comes through simple and humble obedience to the directives of the Almighty. Elder Mark E. Peterson spoke of a growing philosophy in opposition to this principle. He said, "There is the 'new morality' widely heralded. It advocates unrestricted indulgence."[36] On another occasion he taught, "Can we blame God for these modern pestilences as we bring them upon ourselves by our own foolhardy indulgence?"[37] C.S Lewis wrote, "Virtue — even attempted virtue — brings light; indulgence brings fog." (*Mere Christianity*, pg.80) Joseph Smith would have agreed with that statement in light of the 13th Article of Faith which says in part, "...if there is anything virtuous...we seek after these things." It is only through practicing virtue that we can know of the things of the spirit, understand the doctrines of the kingdom, and receive personal revelation from God.

Elder Neal A. Maxwell spoke of enduring to the end as a necessity in our hard journey toward perfection. He said, "Without patient and meek endurance we will learn less, see less, feel less, and hear less. We who are egocentric and impatient shut down much of our receiving capacity."[38] He also wrote:

> Once we have become grounded, rooted, established, and settled, the concluding quality needed is to endure well to the end. Clearly this is much more than merely surviving over the months and the years of life: "And then, if thou endure it well, God shall exalt thee on high; thou shalt triumph over all thy foes." (D&C 121:8)[39]

In the first quote, Elder Maxwell wrote about feeling (i.e., the things of the spirit). C.S. Lewis also wrote about our ability to feel. He said, "The more often he feels without acting, the less he will be able ever to act, and, in the long run, the less he will be able to feel."*(The Screwtape Letters,* pg.57) This implies that if the Holy Ghost, or even the light of Christ, prompts us to do certain things that our Master would have us do, and we ignore those promptings, then we will be less in tune with those promptings the next time around.

Now consider the following excerpt by C.S. Lewis concerning our knowledge of right and wrong, and our frequently choosing the wrong:

Now Christianity, if I have understood the Pauline epistles, does admit that perfect obedience to the moral law, which we find written in our hearts and perceive to be necessary even on the biological level, is not in fact possible to men. This would raise a real difficulty about our responsibility if perfect obedience had any practical relation at all to the lives of most of us. Some degree of obedience which you and I have failed to attain in the last twenty-four hours is certainly possible. The ultimate problem must not be used as one more means of evasion. Most of us are less urgently concerned with the Pauline question than with William Law's simple statement: "if you will here stop and ask yourselves why you are not as pious as the primitive Christians were, your own heart will tell you, that it is neither through ignorance nor inability, but purely because you never thoroughly intended it."[40]

For what is a man profited, if he
shall gain the whole world, and
lose his own soul? or what shall a
man give in exchange for his soul?

— Matthew 16:26

CHAPTER 4

Worldliness and Idols

C.S. Lewis was well acquainted with the danger of worldliness. Perhaps some of us think of worldliness in the most illustrative way as what is portrayed in a beer commercial: carousing people drinking beer, indulging in lusts, and being out of control. Let us observe the writings of C.S. Lewis on the subject. On one occasion he wrote simply, "Aim at Heaven and you will get earth thrown in: aim at earth and you will get neither." *(Mere Christianity, pg.104)*

This statement was probably influenced by the divine words uttered by our Lord when He said, "But seek ye first the kingdom of God, and his righteousness; and all these things shall be added unto you."[41] In *The Book of Mormon* this mortal life on Earth is referred to as a probation — thus we know that it is not here that we should sink our roots. This is merely a proving ground and we are to lay up treasures in heaven, and not on Earth. Because, as C.S. Lewis said, if we aim at earth we will get nothing, and if we aim at heaven we will get heaven and Earth. But, if we are seduced into thinking that this Earth is it, then we are settling for the mess of pottage when we could have had the birthright. If Esau only knew that the birthright included the mess of pottage plus a thousand times more. The Lord revealed to Joseph Smith the following message:

> They seek not the Lord to establish his righteousness, but every man walketh in his own way, and after the image of his own god, whose image is in the likeness of the world, and whose substance is that of an idol, which waxeth old and shall perish in Babylon, even Babylon the great, which shall fall. (D&C 1:16)

And so we do walk in our own way and after the image of our own god. We see how beneficial it is for our own salvation when the Lord tries to beckon us away from these things through the means of missions or church callings or whatever He may use. Consider the following excerpt by C.S. Lewis regarding worldliness and putting our own pursuits above the Lord:

> One great piece of mischief has been done by the modern restriction of the word Temperance to the question of drink. It helps people to forget that you can be just as intemperate about lots of other things. A man who makes his golf or his motor-bicycle the centre of his life, or a woman who devotes all her thoughts to clothes or bridge or her dog, is being just as "intemperate" as someone who gets drunk every evening. Of course, it does not show on the outside so easily: bridge-mania or golf-mania do not make you fall down in the middle of the road. But God is not deceived by externals.[42]

Now keep that in mind as you read this by Hugh Nibley regarding worldliness:

> We have been permitted to come here to go to school, to acquire certain knowledge and take a number of tests to prepare us for greater things hereafter. This whole life, in fact, is "a state of probation" (2 Nephi 2:21). While we are at school our generous patron has provided us with all the necessities of living that we will need to carry us through. Imagine, then, that at the end of the first school year your kind benefactor pays the school a visit. He meets you and asks you how you are doing. "Oh," you say, "I am doing very well, thanks to your bounty." "Are you studying a lot?" "Yes, I am making good progress." "What subjects are you studying?" "Oh, I am studying courses in how to get more lunch." "You study that? All the time?" "Yes. I thought of studying some other subjects. Indeed I would love to study them — some of them are so fascinating! — but after all it's the bread-and-butter courses that count. This is the real world, you know. There is no free lunch." "But my dear boy, I'm providing you with that right now." "Yes, for the time being, and I am grateful — but my purpose in life is to get more and better lunches; I want to go right to the top — the executive suite, the Marriott lunch." "But that is not the work I wanted you to do here," says the patron. "The question in our minds ought to be," says Brigham Young, "what will advance the general interests...and increase intelligence in the minds of the people[?] To do this should be our constant study in preference to how shall we secure that farm or that garden [that is, where the lunch comes from!].... We cannot worship our God in public meeting or kneel down to pray in our families without the images of earthly possessions rising up in our minds to distract them and

make our worship and our prayers unprofitable." Lunch can easily become the one thing the whole office looks forward to all morning: a distraction, a decoy — like sex, it is a passing need that can only too easily become an engrossing obsession. Brigham says, "It is a folly for a man to love...any other kind of property and possessions. One that places his affections upon such things does not understand that they are made for the comfort of the creature, and not for his adoration. They are made to sustain and preserve the body while procuring the knowledge and wisdom that pertain to God and his kingdom [the school motif], in order that we may preserve ourselves, and live forever in his presence."[43]

Throughout his leadership, Brigham Young had much to say about fleeing from worldliness. He counselled the saints in Utah to stay at home and be wise, rather than run off to California when the gold rush hit.[44] He spoke of how the yoke of Christ truly is light, but it is when we try to carry the yoke of Christ and the yoke of the world that it becomes a terrible weight. We must admit this is true. How difficult it is when we try to live the gospel while pursuing the world and its ways simultaneously. Think of the following truth taught by Nephi in *The Book of Mormon*:

> And others will he pacify, and lull them away into carnal security, that they will say: All is well in Zion; yea, Zion prospereth, all is well — and thus the devil cheateth their souls, and leadeth them away carefully down to hell.[45]

C.S. Lewis wrote about the effect of worldliness. He said, "Prosperity knits a man to the World. He feels that he is 'finding his place in it,' while really it is finding its place in him." *(Screwtape Letters)* This concept is similar to what Brigham Young taught when he said:

> Men are greedy for the vain things of this world. In their hearts they are covetous. It is true that the things of this world are designed to make us comfortable, and they make some people as happy as they can be here; but riches can never make the Latter-day Saints happy. Riches of themselves cannot produce permanent happiness; only the Spirit that comes from above can do that.[46]

Material wealth can catch us in a strangle hold that is difficult to shake off. The apostle Paul called wealth a snare. The young rich man who came to Jesus wanted to keep the commandments, but his great riches meant more to him than eternal life. How many of us are in a similar state of mind every hour and every day? Could we, at any given moment, sell everything we own and give the proceeds to the poor? This is a hard doctrine, but Jesus taught it is as hard for a rich man to enter the kingdom of heaven as for a camel to go through the eye of a needle. Whether you believe that this needle's eye spoken of by the Savior is from a literal needle or from a small gate (the gate is of questionable origin) in Israel, the concept is fundamentally the same: heaven is not a place for the rich, but for the poor, especially those who are "poor in spirit" as blessed by the savior.

Many people, including Latter-day Saints, wonder what is so wrong with being rich. The problem is, pride and scorn so often accompany riches, as taught in the following verse from *The Book of Mormon*:

> For they saw and beheld with great sorrow that the people of the church began to be lifted up in the pride of their eyes, and to set their hearts upon riches and upon the vain things of the world, that they began to be scornful, one towards another, and they began to persecute those that did not believe according to their own will and pleasure.[47]

If we think that we can horde wealth and indulge in the things of the world without being tainted and poisoned with the many snares that accompany it, we might as well believe we can play with wild snakes without being bitten. It just comes with the territory.

Then, of course, the usual temptation comes along to observe someone in the Bible who was rich, yet went on to eternal life, such as Abraham. Before we are too quick to justify our indulgences by his apparent riches, let us remember a few things: Abraham went out every night and looked for poor people to bring home with him and feed. He was willing to sacrifice his son — how much easier would it have been for him had the Lord merely asked for his wealth, rather than his own son!?

From *The Screwtape Letters*, C.S. Lewis offers an insight on the snares of worldliness in relation to temptations from the devil. The context is taken from a letter from Screwtape (a master tempter) to Wormwood (his nephew, and a junior tempter). He writes:

> All these, as I find from the record office, are thoroughly reliable people; steady, consistent scoffers and worldlings who without any spectacular crimes are progressing quietly and comfortably towards Our Father's house.[48]

The "Father" spoken of is the father of lies, Lucifer. C.S. Lewis describes remarkably well in the above excerpt those in "the great and spacious building" that Lehi described from a revelatory dream. This kind of person is not only worldly but scoffs at those trying to live the Christlike life. From the same book as mentioned above, Screwtape makes this observation to his nephew: "One of our best weapons, contented worldliness, is rendered useless. In wartime not even a human can believe that he is going to live forever." *(The Screwtape Letters,* pg.33) He also wrote, "In peace we can make many of them ignore good and evil entirely; in danger, the issue is forced upon them in a guise to which even we cannot blind them." *(The Screwtape Letters,* pg.104) Compare this with the words of Ezra Taft Benson, as follows:

> We must make sure that freedom means more to our youth than just peace. We must make sure that freedom means more to our youth than just security. We must make sure that freedom means more to our youth than just selfish gain. We must emphasize the need of character in the citizens of America.[49]

Now this brings up another principle; worldliness is hard to indulge in and maintain when our lives are being severely disrupted by things such as war or pain or tragedy. Perhaps the Lord uses these things (while evil in themselves) as tools in uprooting us from the world and planting us in holier gardens.

Another temptation that usually floats around, and somehow gets into the air we breathe, is that we can make the world into heaven. Think upon C.S. Lewis' comment regarding this philosophy:

> So inveterate is their appetite for Heaven, that our best method, at this stage, of attaching them to Earth is to make them believe that Earth can be turned into Heaven at some future date by politics or eugenics or "science" or psychology or what not. Real worldliness is a work of time — assisted, of course, by pride, for we teach them to describe the creeping death as Good Sense or Maturity or Experience.[50]

Again, compare the above with the words of Ezra Taft Benson:

> Joseph was put in prison because he put God first. If we were faced with a similar choice, where would we place our first loyalty? Can we put God ahead of security, peace, passions, wealth, and the honors of men?[51]

27

Now this from David O. McKay:

> The poor in spirit are they who are conscious of their destitu-
> tion — not of worldly possessions but of heavenly riches. Those
> who experience this condition run counter to them who arro-
> gantly manifest pride in personal accomplishments or acquired
> possessions.[52]

Often times we slip into worldliness because of peer pressure, and C.S. Lewis understood this well. He wrote on one occasion:

> I am credibly informed that young humans now sometimes
> suppress an incipient taste for classical music or good literature
> because it might prevent their Being Like Folks; that people who
> would really wish to be — and are offered the Grace which would
> enable them to be — honest, chaste, or temperate refuse it. To accept
> might make them Different, might offend against the Way of Life,
> take them out of Togetherness, impair their Integration with the
> Group. They might (horror of horrors!) become individuals.[53]

Quite a succinct commentary on the world of peer pressure, isn't it? Compare that with the following from Neal A. Maxwell:

> WINSTON: I'm struck again and again by how circumstances
> and social pressure can also keep the individual's faith from flow-
> ering fully and openly. Listen to these verses from Nephi: "After
> they had tasted of the fruit they were ashamed, because of those
> that were scoffing at them; and they fell away into forbidden paths
> and were lost." (1 Nephi 8:28) Peer pressure through the ages![54]

The worldly always have been and always will be mockers. They have always been adept in the field of scorn — it is one of Satan's most potent tools, and has turned many a hopeful away from the Tree of Life when they were so close to partaking fully.

I don't know if this quite fits here, but I've got to mention it anyway. Many Catholics and Protestants wonder why L.D.S. churches do not have crucifixes, paintings, sculptures, or other visible symbols of our Lord. Here is another letter from Screwtape to Wormwood on the tactics of drawing humans away from the Lord:

> I have known cases where what the patient called his "God"
> was actually located — up and to the left at the corner of the

bedroom ceiling, or inside his own head, or in a crucifix on the wall. But whatever the nature of the composite object, you must keep him praying to *it* — to the thing that he has made, not to the Person who has made him.[55]

It's probably easier than we may think to slip into the trap of worshipping representations of God rather than the true and living God Himself.

Because strait is the gate,
and narrow is the way, which
leadeth unto life, and few
there be that find it.

— 3 Nephi 14:14

CHAPTER 5

Eternal Progression or Digression?

It must be the nature of human souls in mortality to be in a constant state of flux. We are always changing — emotionally, physically, spiritually, intellectually. We couldn't stop this change even if we wanted to. Of course, just because we are changing does not always mean we are improving; that is up to us. Even though God in heaven is "the same yesterday, today, and forever," the mortal Messiah changed from "grace to grace" and "received not a fullness at first." Adolf Hitler was probably not evil at the age of seven. But he retrogressed and persisted in his wickedness until a monster began to take shape. C.S. Lewis believed, as we do, in the concept of eternal progression. He knew that it is really a matter of choice. Every choice we make, small or large, adds up to make our character and our destiny. He wrote:

> People often think of Christian morality as a kind of bargain in which God says, "If you keep a lot of rules I'll reward you, and if you don't I'll do the other thing." I do not think that is the best way of looking at it. I would much rather say that every time you make a choice you are turning the central part of you, the part of you that chooses, into something a little different from what it was before. And taking your life as a whole, with all your innumerable choices, all your life long you are slowly turning this central thing either into a heavenly creature or into a hellish creature: either into a creature that is in harmony with God, and with other creatures, and with itself, or else into one that is in a state of war and hatred with God, and with its fellow-creatures, and with itself. To be the one kind of creature is heaven: that is, it is joy and peace and knowledge and power. To be the other means madness, horror, idiocy, rage, impotence, and eternal loneliness. Each of us at each moment is progressing to the one state or the other.[56]

His words are not only accurate, but eloquent as well. Each of our Final Outcomes are now in the making. What we do tomorrow and next week will contribute in some way to that. C.S. Lewis also said, "All mortals tend to turn into the thing they are pretending to be."[57] In Proverbs we learn, "For as he thinketh in his heart, so [is] he..." (Proverbs 23:7) This idea also sheds light on our state in the afterlife. Latter-day Saints understand the phrase "eternal damnation" more clearly than general Christians, because the Lord has revealed that it has to do with our eternal progression, which is halted within the parameters of damnation. Exaltation, however, is the continuation of joy and power and family forever. Marion G. Romney spoke of the relationship between individual choices and our eternal progression in the following way:

> And finally, when the issues are determined, whether we stand with the winners or the losers, of this we may be sure: To make the proper choice on any issue is of far more importance to us personally than is the immediate outcome of the issue upon which we make a decision. The choices we make will affect the scope of our agency in the future. As of now, we have the right of decision. What we will have tomorrow depends upon how we decide today.[58]

Thus, our choices are of the utmost importance. A good choice today may expand the possibility of our choices next month, as may a poor choice today restrict our choices in the future. Another key doctrine that C.S. Lewis understood was the old idea that the bigger they are (in a spiritual sense), the harder they fall. He once wrote: "Of all bad men, religious bad men are the worst. Of all created beings the wickedest is one who originally stood in the immediate presence of God."[59] Alma stated it in this way:

> And thus we can plainly discern that after a people have been once enlightened by the Spirit of God and have had great knowledge of things pertaining to righteousness, and then have fallen away into sin and transgression, they become more hardened, and thus their state becomes worse than though they had never known these things. (Alma 24:30)

C.S. Lewis understood this and put it into these words:

> It seems that there is a general rule in the moral universe which may be formulated "The higher, the more in danger." The "average sensual man" who is sometimes unfaithful to his wife, sometimes tipsy, always a little selfish, now and then (within the

law) a trifle sharp in his deals, is certainly, by ordinary standards, a 'lower' type than the man whose soul is filled with some great Cause, to which he will subordinate his appetites, his fortune, and even his safety. But it is out of the second man that something really fiendish can be made; an Inquisitor, a Member of the Committee of Public Safety. It is great men, potential saints, not little men, who become merciless fanatics.[60]

The Lord taught, "For of him unto whom much is given much is required; and he who sins against the greater light shall receive the greater condemnation."[61] C.S. Lewis also said the following:

> I think we must fully face the fact that when Christianity does not make a man very much better, it makes him very much worse. It is, paradoxically, dangerous to draw nearer to God.[62]

And this:

> There is either a warning or an encouragement here for every one of us. If you are a nice person — if virtue comes easily to you — beware! Much is expected from those to whom much is given.[63]

In our own church history we have seen this time and again. William Law was at one time an apostle of Jesus Christ, in the closest confidence of Joseph Smith. Yet he fell away and became one of the vilest enemies of the church — it is even possible that he was among the mob that killed the Prophet. Joseph Smith taught that once someone ascended to great spiritual heights, had the heavens opened to him, and had marvelous manifestations of the Holy Ghost, if that person then fell away, he would fight against God, persecute the saints, and thirst for their blood.[64]

Another important principle of the gospel, taught most forcefully by Nephi, and understood by C.S. Lewis, is that of not placing our trust in the arm of flesh, where matters of salvation are concerned. Nephi said:

> O Lord, I have trusted in thee, and I will trust in thee forever. I will not put my trust in the arm of flesh; for I know that cursed is he that putteth his trust in the arm of flesh. Yea, cursed is he that putteth his trust in man or maketh flesh his arm....Cursed is he that putteth his trust in man, or maketh flesh his arm, or shall hearken unto the precepts of men, save their precepts shall be given by the power of the Holy Ghost. (2 Nephi 4:34, 2 Nephi 28:31)

C.S. Lewis wrote:

> But we must not remain babies. We must go on to recognise the real Giver. It is madness not to. Because, if we do not, we shall be relying on human beings. And that is going to let us down. The best of them will make mistakes; all of them will die. We must be thankful to all the people who have helped us. We must honour them and love them. But never, never pin your whole faith on any human being: not if he is the best and wisest in the whole world. There are lots of nice things you can do with sand; but do not try building a house on it.[65]

This was a stumbling block for the early saints also. How many times did a prominent man in the church apostatize — even apostles? As for any saints that trusted in them, or leaned upon them in matters relating to their spiritual well-being, they often fell away. Only those firmly rooted in Christ, who had not put their trust in the arm of flesh, did not fall away.

We know that temptation often hits hardest when we are weak or afflicted or otherwise downcast in spirit. The Lord taught His followers in Israel, "Watch and pray, that ye enter not into temptation: the spirit indeed [is] willing, but the flesh [is] weak."[66] It makes sense that Satan would try to attack us when we are weak rather than strong. C.S. Lewis understood this truth, as well. In *The Screwtape Letters*, Screwtape is writing advice to his less experienced nephew Wormwood. He writes:

> The attack has a much better chance of success when the man's whole inner world is drab and cold and empty. And it is also to be noted that the Trough sexuality is subtly different in quality from that of the Peak — much less likely to lead to the mild-and-water phenomenon which the humans call "being in love," much more easily drawn into perversions, much less contaminated by those generous and imaginative and even spiritual concomitants which often render human sexuality so disappointing. It is the same with other desires of the flesh. You are much more likely to make your man a sound drunkard by pressing drink on him as an anodyne when he is dull and weary than by encouraging him to use it as a means of merriment among his friends when he is happy and expansive.[67]

We have only to look at our own past (and probably not very far back, either) to find evidence of this principle in our own lives. When we get discouraged, or even close to despair, we tend to lose some of our strength and immunity against sin. Our resistance is lowered, our shields fall, and sin awaits at the door. We must always be on our guard.

In relation to our progression, a key part of the whole thing is this tough mortality in which we now live. It was not meant to be easy, for we are here to be tested and to grow. C.S. Lewis has left us with a wise insight on this matter. He wrote:

> I used to think it was a 'cruel' doctrine to say that troubles and sorrows were 'punishments'. But I find in practice that when you are in trouble, the moment you regard it as a 'punishment', it becomes easier to bear. If you think of this world as a place intended simply for our happiness, you find it quite intolerable: think of it as a place of training and correction and it's not so bad.[68]

We must reach certain levels of growth, righteousness, and sanctification in order to attain the equivalent levels of glory and mansions in the next life. Those who are not obedient to the commandments of God, cannot expect to inherit the same glories as Abraham or Nephi. The Lord revealed to Joseph Smith the following revelatory truths

> For he who is not able to abide the law of a celestial kingdom cannot abide a celestial glory.
>
> And he who cannot abide the law of a terrestrial kingdom cannot abide a terrestrial glory.
>
> And he who cannot abide the law of a telestial kingdom cannot abide a telestial glory; therefore he is not meet for a kingdom of glory. Therefore he must abide a kingdom which is not a kingdom of glory.[69]

The greater the laws of God that we are able to obey, the greater potential for us for blessings connected with those laws. And, when we sin against greater laws, there is greater condemnation. Again, from the *Doctrine and Covenants* we have:

> That which breaketh a law, and abideth not by law, but seeketh to become a law unto itself, and willeth to abide in sin, and altogether abideth in sin, cannot be sanctified by law, neither by mercy, justice, nor judgment. Therefore, they must remain filthy still. (D&C 88:35)

This verse illustrates powerfully the principle of agency. Everything we may become — our entire potential — rests squarely on our choices in relation to the light and knowledge we have from God.

Here I must go off on a tangent for a moment. C.S. Lewis wrote in one of his books of something that is mentioned briefly in scripture, but only in the House of the Lord can we understand it more fully. C.S. Lewis wrote:

> But it is also said "To him that overcometh I will give a white stone, and in the stone a new name written, which no man knoweth saving he that receiveth it." What can be more a man's own than this new name which even in eternity remains a secret between God and him? And what shall we take this secrecy to mean? Surely, that each of the redeemed shall forever know and praise some one aspect of the divine beauty better than any other creature can.[70]

Interesting, isn't it? He didn't have the knowledge that we as Latter-day Saints do, but he must have felt that there was something unique and wonderful in the doctrine. In our day, the Lord has revealed this on the subject:

> And a white stone is given to each of those who come into the celestial kingdom, whereon is a new name written, which no man knoweth save he that receiveth it. The new name is the key word.[71]

C.S. Lewis was really seeking the truth, and I don't believe he was afraid of it when he found it. He knew and understood more than most outside the fold of the restored gospel concerning eternal progression, and many of the purposes of the Lord, as evidenced by excerpts we have read. To conclude this chapter, let us observe the words of King Benjamin, who sums up the whole matter rather succinctly:

> But this much I can tell you, that if ye do not watch yourselves, and your thoughts, and your words, and your deeds, and observe the commandments of God, and continue in the faith of what ye have heard concerning the coming of our Lord, even unto the end of your lives, ye must perish. And now, O man, remember, and perish not. (Mosiah 4:30)

"For I am not ashamed of the gospel of Christ: for it is the power of God unto salvation to every one that believeth; to the Jew first, and also to the Greek."

— Romans 1:16

CHAPTER 6

On Being a Christian

C.S. Lewis had much to say about Christianity; in fact, he wrote an entire book on the subject and titled it *Mere Christianity*. He believed that within this broad, encompassing faith called Christianity, there are definite truths that cannot be ignored or watered down; that the essence of Christianity is positively true regardless of myths and false doctrines that have arisen under the pretense of Christianity. Many of his ideas are amazingly similar to those truths we have in the restored gospel. Here is an excerpt from C.S. Lewis to start us off:

> There is a story about a schoolboy who was asked what he thought God was like. He replied that, as far as he could make out, God was "The sort of person who is always snooping round to see if anyone is enjoying himself and then trying to stop it." And I am afraid that is the sort of idea that the word Morality raises in a good many people's minds: something that interferes, something that stops you having a good time. In reality, moral rules are directions for running the human machine. Every moral rule is there to prevent a breakdown, or a strain, or a friction, in the running of that machine. That is why these rules at first seem to be constantly interfering with our natural inclination. When you are being taught how to use any machine, the instructor keeps on saying, "No, don't do it like that," because, of course, there are all sorts of things that look all right and seem to you the natural way of treating the machine, but do not really work.[72]

He knew better than to believe in the idea mentioned above of a God who doesn't want anyone to enjoy life — that He exists to make sure we don't have any fun. God desires our eternal joy, but so many immediate pleasures will, if not properly controlled — and some-times abstained from — destroy for us our potential of that eternal joy that our Heavenly Father wants us to obtain. Lewis understood the divine and absolutely necessary purposes of moral rules. They are not to restrict us and make us miserable, so much as to keep us out of the ditch and on a straight course for eternal life. He had a very good grasp on what the true gospel of Christ is and what it is not. He wrote:

> The second thing to get clear is that Christianity has not, and does not profess to have, a detailed political programme for applying "Do as you would be done by" to a particular society at a particular moment. It could not have. It is meant for all men at all times and the particular programme which suited one place or time would not suit another. And, anyhow, that is not how Christianity works. When it tells you to feed the hungry it does not give you lessons in cookery. When it tells you to read the Scriptures it does not give you lessons in Hebrew and Greek, or even in English grammar. It was never intended to replace or supersede the ordi-nary human arts and sciences: it is rather a director which will set them all to the right jobs, and a source of energy which will give them all new life, if only they will put themselves at its disposal.[73]

We know and understand through our own prophets and apostles what C.S. Lewis spoke of above. The true gospel is a universal and all-encompassing plan that is not limited to cultures or time frames. It is meant to save and bring happiness to all who will embrace it. The true gospel has existed as long as the universe, and conforms to all truth. Think of the excerpt above in relation to the following truth taught in the *Doctrine and Covenants*:

> Verily I say, men should be anxiously engaged in a good cause, and do many things of their own free will, and bring to pass much righteousness;[74]

That is really the whole message of Christianity: to be anxiously engaged in a good cause. But, it gives only general guidelines on how to accomplish this, the rest being up to our discretion. In the next passage, you will see what C.S. Lewis thought about becoming a Christian, and what to expect when we embark on that great journey the Lord has prepared for us:

> If you are thinking of becoming a Christian, I warn you are embarking on something which is going to take the whole of you, brains and all. But, fortunately, it works the other way round.

> Anyone who is honestly trying to be a Christian will soon find his intelligence being sharpened: one of the reasons why it needs no special education to be a Christian is that Christianity is an education itself. That is why an uneducated believer like Bunyan was able to write a book that has astonished the whole world.[75]

This excerpt is packed with profound gems of truth — quite remarkable for a nonmember to pick up on. He speaks of Christianity taking the whole of us. Think of the law of consecration. He speaks of our intelligence being sharpened. Think of the Lord's promise that our minds and bodies will be renewed in the midst of doing His work. He speaks of Christians needing no special education. This is quite familiar to us because *The Book of Mormon* says the learned will reject the truths within it. Also, the Lord, in the *Doctrine and Covenants* makes clear the fact that the gospel will be preached by the weak and simple of the Earth. When I read the last sentence of the above excerpt, I immediately thought of Joseph Smith. What if you were to rewrite his sentence in this way: "That is why an uneducated believer like Joseph Smith was able to translate a book that has astonished the whole world."

Apparently, C.S. Lewis heard some people argue against Christianity by saying it is supposed to be an altruistic system of self-denial, service for others, and complete charity, yet the whole religion is based upon rewards and punishments. Isn't this, they argued, just a mercenary affair? Here is his reply:

> We must not be troubled by unbelievers when they say that this promise of reward makes the Christian life a mercenary affair. There are different kinds of rewards. There is the reward which has no natural connection with the things you do to earn it, and is quite foreign to the desires that ought to accompany those things. Money is not the natural reward of love; that is why we call a man mercenary if he marries a woman for the sake of her money. But marriage is the proper reward for a real lover, and he is not mercenary for desiring it. A general who fights well in order to get a peerage is mercenary; a general who fights for victory is not, victory being the proper reward of battle as marriage is the proper reward of love. The proper rewards are not simply tacked on to the activity for which they are given, but are the activity itself in consummation.[76]

The savior laid down his life and suffered immeasurably for us because He had the kind of love with no strings attached. He desired our eternal well-being more than his initial comfort. He was willing to suffer and die so that we might not suffer — and live. He laid down His life for His friends, and ultimately we must take this pure love of Christ upon us completely, and be willing to do for others what He did for us. That is what it is all about.

One doctrine that has been almost universally denied in our day by Christianity as a whole is the concept of *revelation;* that God still speaks to man, and has not left us alone. Even though his own church believed to the contrary, C.S. Lewis believed that revelation in true Christianity is essential. He said, "There is nothing irrational in exercising other powers than our reason.... It is rational not to reason, or not to limit oneself to reason, in the wrong place; and the more rational a man is the better he knows this...." *(Mere Christianity)* He also wrote:

> We should expect to find in the Church an element which unbelievers will call irrational and which believers will call supra-rational. There ought to be something in it opaque to our reason though not contrary to it...The Church of England can remain a church only if she retains this opaque element. If we abandon that, if we retain only what can be justified by standards of prudence and convenience at the bar of enlightened common sense, then we exchange revelation for that old wraith Natural Religion. *(Mere Christianity)*

Now let's look at an interesting philosophical dilemma in relation to Christianity. When God gave the Ten Commandments he said, "Thou shalt not kill." Yet He commanded Nephi to kill Laban. This was not in the midst of a war, and it wasn't even self-defense. How is it justified? Recall the story:

> And it came to pass that I was constrained by the Spirit that I should kill Laban; but I said in my heart: Never at any time have I shed the blood of man. And I shrunk and would that I might not slay him. And the Spirit said unto me again: Behold the Lord hath delivered him into thy hands. Yea, and I also knew that he had sought to take away mine own life; yea, and he would not hearken unto the commandments of the Lord; and he also had taken away our property. And it came to pass that the Spirit said unto me again: Slay him, for the Lord hath delivered him into thy hands; Behold the Lord slayeth the wicked to bring forth his righteous purposes. It is better that one man should perish than that a nation should dwindle and perish in unbelief. And now, when I, Nephi, had heard these words, I remembered the words of the Lord which he spake unto me in the wilderness, saying that: Inasmuch as thy seed shall keep my commandments, they shall prosper in the land of promise. Yea, and I also thought that they could not keep the commandments of the Lord according to the law of Moses, save

they should have the law. And I also knew that the law was engraven upon the plates of brass. And again, I knew that the Lord had delivered Laban into my hands for this cause — that I might obtain the records according to his commandments. Therefore I did obey the voice of the Spirit, and took Laban by the hair of the head, and I smote off his head with his own sword. (1 Nephi 4:10-18)

Although C.S. Lewis never read *The Book of Mormon,* he had obviously considered this dilemma. With that in mind, read the following that he wrote:

> The whole system is, so to speak, calculated for the clash between good men and bad men, and the good fruits of fortitude, patience, pity and forgiveness for which the cruel man is permitted to be cruel, presuppose that the good man ordinarily continues to seek simple good. I say "ordinarily" because a man is sometimes entitled to hurt (or even, in my opinion, to kill) his fellow, but only where the necessity is urgent and the good to be attained obvious, and usually (though not always) when he who inflicts the pain has a definite authority to do so — a parent's authority derived from nature, a magistrate's or soldier's derived from civil society, or as surgeon's derive, most often, from the patient.[77]

Lewis says killing is justified if (1) the necessity is urgent and the good to be attained obvious. "Yea, and I also knew that he had sought to take away mine own life…It is better that one man should perish than that a nation should dwindle and perish in unbelief…Yea, and I also thought that they could not keep the commandments of the Lord according to the law of Moses, save they should have the law. And I also knew that the law was engraven upon the plates of brass." (2) When he who inflicts the pain has a definite authority to do so. "And the Spirit said unto me again: Behold the Lord hath delivered him into thy hands….And it came to pass that the Spirit said unto me again: Slay him, for the Lord hath delivered him into thy hands; Behold the Lord slayeth the wicked to bring forth his righteous purposes…I knew that the Lord had delivered Laban into my hands for this cause — that I might obtain the records according to his commandments. Therefore I did obey the voice of the Spirit…"

Now a word about humility. Christianity unequivocally demands our humility. That is an essential ingredient to lasting happiness, because it is the antidote and the antithesis of pride. Here is what C.S. Lewis has said about it, and also about some of the myths that have arisen in conjunction with the concept of humility:

Perhaps you have imagined that this humility in the saints is a pious illusion at which God smiles. That is a most dangerous error. It is theoretically dangerous, because it makes you identify a virtue (i.e., a perfection) with an illusion (i.e., an imperfection), which must be nonsense. It is practically dangerous because it encourages a man to mistake his first insights into his own corruption for the first beginnings of a halo round his own silly head. No, depend upon it; when the saints say that they — even they — are vile, they are recording truth with scientific accuracy.[78]

Of humility, he also said, "Perfect humility dispenses with modesty."[79] True humility is neither "pious illusion" nor false modesty. No, humility is a divine attribute. Even God, the creator and ruler of all things, is humble. After Christ visited Moroni anciently, Moroni recorded that Jesus spoke with him "in plain humility."[80]

Jesus taught, "Greater love hath no man than this, that a man lay down his life for his friends."[81] C.S. Lewis formulated an opinion on martyrs that is worth mentioning. Many great men and women have laid down their lives in the cause of Christianity. Some of the greatest we readily know of: Jesus, Joseph Smith, Peter, Abinadi, and John the Baptist. It seems to be a common thread and a consistent theme within Christianity. C.S. Lewis wrote the following about martyrdom:

Hence as suicide is the typical expression of the stoic spirit, and battle of the warrior spirit, martyrdom always remains the supreme enacting and perfection of Christianity. This great action has been initiated for us, done on our behalf, exemplified for our imitation, and inconceivably communicated to all believers, by Christ on Calvary.[82]

Bruce R. McConkie also commented on martyrdom. He wrote the following:

Martyrs of religion are found in every age in which there have been both righteous and wicked people on earth. Christ himself was a martyr who voluntarily laid down his life, according to the Father's plan, that immortality and eternal life might become available for his brethren. (John 10:10-18) "Greater love hath no man than this, that a man lay down his life for his friends." (John 15:13)[83]

He said also:

Many apostles, prophets, and saints have been martyred for the gospel cause. (Matt. 23:29-33; Luke 11:47-51; Acts 7; 22:20; Hel. 13:24-28; D&C 135) The Prophet and Patriarch of this dispensation laid down their lives in the gospel cause, as literally thousands of others have done. Men, women, and children, young and old, weak and strong, sick and well, were driven by the thousands from Missouri and Illinois, many to early and untimely deaths as a direct result of the persecutions and diseases thus heaped upon them. Is a saint any less a martyr who is driven from a sick bed into blizzards to freeze and die than he would have been had an assassin's bullet brought merciful death in a brief destroying moment?[84]

An age-old dispute in Christianity is over whether we are saved by grace or by works. In the Bible, James spoke about the great importance of works, and Paul of grace. Where does that leave us? The question continues today. Fortunately, Nephi answered the question for us when he wrote, "...for we know that it is by grace that we are saved, after all we can do." (2 Nephi 25:23) C.S Lewis also understood this adeptly. He wrote:

> Christians have often disputed as to whether what leads the Christian home is good actions, or Faith in Christ. I have no right really to speak on such a difficult question, but it does seem to me like asking which blade in a pair of scissors is most necessary. A serious moral effort is the only thing that will bring you to the point where you throw up the sponge. Faith in Christ is the only thing to save you from despair at that point: and out of that Faith in Him good actions must inevitably come.[85]

He speaks of "a serious moral effort." How else but by this serious effort can we perfect ourselves or become sanctified? On the other hand, it is not by our own efforts that we are redeemed, but through the atoning sacrifice of our Lord.

Another aspect of Christianity that C.S. Lewis believed to be fundamental (and which we know to be fundamental!) is that personal purity and righteousness is a prerequisite for us to come to *know* God, and to be in tune with the truth. He wrote:

> ...while in other sciences the instruments you use are things external to yourself (things like microscopes and telescopes), the instrument through which you see God is your whole self. And if a man's self is not kept clean and bright, his glimpse of God will be blurred — like the Moon seen through a dirty telescope. That is why horrible nations have horrible religions: they have been looking at God through a dirty lens.[86]

The scriptures teach us that if we sin against the light that we have, then the Spirit departs from us; and when that happens, the adversary is able to exercise his power over us. This is when, as C.S. Lewis said, we begin to look at God "through a dirty lens." Compare this idea with something that Elder Dallin H. Oaks once taught:

> Each of us has a personal lens through which we view the world. Our lens gives its special tint to all we see. It can also suppress some features and emphasize others. It can reveal things otherwise invisible. Through the lens of spirituality, we can know "the things of God" by "the Spirit of God" (1 Corinthians 2:11). As the Apostle Paul taught, such things are "foolishness" to the "natural man." He cannot see them "because they are spiritually discerned" (1 Corinthians 2:14).[87]

Another fundamental part of the true gospel of Jesus Christ is the Temple — the house of the Lord. C.S. Lewis had a surprising awareness of this doctrine, at least in a roundabout sort of way. He once wrote in a letter to an unnamed lady, "You have gone into the Temple…and found Him, as always, there." *(Letters of C.S. Lewis)* We must remember, though, that this is taken more or less out of context — we don't really know what he was referring to. In scripture, when there has been a prophet God wanted to speak with, and no temple nearby, a mountaintop was used for this sacred and holy communion. Here is another very interesting excerpt by C.S. Lewis from his *Chronicles of Narnia* series:

> 'Here on the mountain I have spoken to you clearly: I will not often do so down in Narnia. Here on the mountain, the air is clear and your mind is clear; as you drop down into Narnia, the air will thicken. Take great care that it does not confuse your mind. And the signs which you have learned here will not look at all as you expect them to look, when you meet them there. That is why it is so important to know them by heart and pay no attention to appearance. Remember the signs and believe the signs. Nothing else matters.'[88]

This almost makes you wonder if C.S. Lewis has been to the Temple. The above passage is filled with powerful symbolism that hints of the Temple, from the clear air at the top of the mountain, to the signs to remember.

One of the surprising and ironic things about C.S. Lewis, in all of his gospel knowledge and awareness, is that he used to be an atheist. Perhaps it makes perfect sense. Maybe he is much like the sons of Mosiah or Saul of Tarsus — they were atheists and worse — only to turn around and become great soldiers in the Lord's army. C.S. Lewis wrote of his past atheism in the following way:

Not many years ago when I was an atheist, if anyone had asked me, "Why do you not believe in God?" my reply would have run something like this: "Look at the universe we live in. By far the greatest part of it consists of empty space, completely dark and unimaginably cold. The bodies which move in this space are so few and so small in comparison with the space itself that even if every one of them were known to be crowded as full as it could hold with perfectly happy creatures, it would still be difficult to believe that life and happiness were more than a by-product to the power that made the universe. As it is, however, the scientists think it likely that very few of the suns of space — perhaps none of them except our own — have any planets; ... And what is [Earth] like while it lasts? It is so arranged that all the forms of it can live only by preying upon one another. In the lower forms this process entails only death, but in the higher there appears a new quality called consciousness which enables it to be attended with pain. The creatures cause pain by being born, and live by inflicting pain, and in pain they mostly die. In the most complex of all the creatures, Man, yet another quality appears, which we call reason, whereby he is able to foresee his own pain which henceforth is preceded with acute mental suffering, and to foresee his own death while keenly desiring permanence. It also enables men by a hundred ingenious contrivances to inflict a great deal more pain than they otherwise could have done on one another and on the irrational creatures. This power they have exploited to the full. Their history is largely a record of crime, war, disease, and terror, with just sufficient happiness interposed to give them, while it lasts, an agonized apprehension of losing it, and when it is lost, the poignant misery of remembering."[89]

Compare his words with those of Neal A. Maxwell:

Imbedded in the profound truths of the Restoration is relief from the painful dilemmas which have caused some to stumble and fall. Significant answers are now available to cruel questions such as "If God is good and omnipotent, why does He permit suffering and evil?" In response thereto we learn important truths about the combined consequences of misused agency and about the role of divine tutoring. Some challenges built into life are "common to all men. "Infant mortality is not left as a dangling dilemma. And in the just plan of God there are provisions for those who do not hear the gospel in mortality. These and other answers underscore the ultimate justice and mercy of God.[90]

Whereas C.S. Lewis used to hold to atheism as a staunch and realistic philosophy, he now holds it in contempt. He once said, "The notion that everyone would like Christianity to be true, and therefore all atheists are brave men who have accepted the defeat of all their deepest desires, is simply impudent nonsense."[91] Here is another perspective from him on atheism, and his emergence into Christianity and truth:

> If what you want is an argument against Christianity (and I well remember how eagerly I looked for such arguments when I began to be afraid it was true) you can easily find some stupid and unsatisfactory Christian and say, "So there's your boasted new man! Give me the old kind." But if once you have begun to see that Christianity is on other grounds probable, you will know in your heart that this is only evading the issue. What can you ever really know of other people's souls — of their temptations, their opportunities, their struggles? One soul in the whole creation you do know: and it is the only one whose fate is placed in your hands. If there is a God, you are, in a sense, alone with Him. You cannot put Him off with speculations about your next door neighbors or memories of what you have read in books. What will all that chatter and hearsay count (will you even be able to remember it?) when the anaesthetic fog which we call "nature" or "the real world" fades away and the Presence in which you have always stood becomes palpable, immediate, and unavoidable?[92]

He speaks of spiritual things and afterlife as though they were the actual reality, and that what we now call reality as "anaesthetic fog." And so it is. The apostle Paul spoke of this uncertain mortality when he said, "For now we see through a glass, darkly; but then face to face: now I know in part; but then shall I know even as also I am known." (1 Cor. 13:12)

C.S. Lewis tried to figure out the essence of Christianity — what it is *really* all about. He does so and relates it to politics and government as follows:

> May I come back to what I said before? This is the whole of Christianity. There is nothing else. It is so easy to get muddled about that. It is easy to think that the Church has a lot of different objects — education, building, missions, holding services. Just as it is easy to think the State has a lot of different objects — military, political, economic, and what not. But in a way things are much simpler than that. The State exists simply to promote and to protect the ordinary happiness of human beings in this life. A husband and wife chatting over a fire, a couple of friends having a game of darts in a pub, a man reading a book in his own room or digging in his own garden — that is what the State is there for. And unless they are helping to increase and prolong and protect such moments, all the laws, parliaments, armies, courts, police,

economics, etc., are simply a waste of time. In the same way the Church exists for nothing else but do draw men into Christ, to make them little Christs. If they are not doing that, all the cathedrals, clergy, missions, sermons, even the Bible itself, are simply a waste of time. God became Man for no other purpose. It is even doubtful you know whether the whole universe was created for any other purpose. It says in the Bible that the whole universe was made for Christ and that everything is to be gathered together in Him. I do not suppose any of us can understand how this will happen as regards the whole universe. We do not know what (if anything) lives in the parts of it that are millions of miles away from this Earth. Even on this Earth we do not know how it applies to things other than men. After all, that is what you would expect. We have been shown the plan only in so far as it concerns ourselves.[93]

Now compare these ideas with the words of Ezra Taft Benson in the following two excerpts:

The founders of this republic had deeply spiritual beliefs. Their concept of man had a solidly religious foundation. They believed "it is not right that any man should be in bondage one to another." (D&C 101:79) They believed that men were capable of self-government and that it was the job of government to protect freedom and foster private initiative.[94]

I believe that God has endowed men with certain inalienable rights as set forth in the Declaration of Independence and that no legislature and no majority, however great, may morally limit or destroy these; that the sole function of government is to protect life, liberty, and property, and anything more than this is usurpation and oppression.[95]

Just as the role of government is to protect its citizens and foster peace and happiness, the role of religion is to bring us back to our Heavenly Father and partake of eternal life with Him.

Another doctrine important to Christianity is that of not judging other people. In C.S. Lewis' masterpiece *The Screwtape Letters*, Screwtape is sending advice to his nephew Wormwood on how to best tempt and destroy their mortal "patients." In one of these correspondences, Screwtape is extolling the benefits of getting the patient to judge others while at church. The passage is both amusing and insightful. It reads:

When he gets to his pew and looks round him he sees just that selection of his neighbors whom he has hitherto avoided. You want to lean pretty heavily on those neighbors. Make his mind flit to and fro between an expression like "the body of Christ" and the actual faces in the next pew. It matters very little, or course, what kind of people that next pew really contains. You may know one of them to be a great warrior on the Enemy's side. No matter. Your patient, thanks to Our Father Below, is a fool. Provided that any of those neighbors sing out of tune, or have boots that squeak, or double chins, or odd clothes, the patient will quite easily believe that their religion must therefore be somehow ridiculous. At his present stage, you see, he has an idea of "Christians" in his mind which he supposes to be spiritual but which, in fact, is largely pictorial.[96]

Here is another segment of a letter from Screwtape to Wormwood:

I have been writing hitherto on the assumption that the people in the next pew afford no rational ground for disappointment. Of course, if they do — if the patient knows that the woman with the absurd hat is a fanatical bridgeplayer or the man with squeaky boots a miser and an extortioner — then your task is so much the easier. All you then have to do is to keep out of his mind the question "If I, being what I am, can consider than I am in some sense a Christian, why should the different vices of those people in the next pew prove that their religion is mere hypocrisy and convention?"[97]

This judgmental attitude can creep into the best of people subtly and smoothly. It can undermine our humility and creep pride into our souls. Of this, Elder Dallin Oaks taught:

Our attitudes determine how we evaluate our life's experiences. They determine how we evaluate ourselves. They also govern how we look at other people. Are we inclined to judge an eternal soul by the appearance of an earthly body? Do we see the beautiful soul of a brother or sister, or do we only see that person's earthly tabernacle? Bodies can be distorted by handicap, twisted by injury, or worn by age. But if we can learn to see the inner man and woman, we will be seeing as God sees, and loving as he loves.[98]

Elder Mark E. Petersen taught a similar principle:

A return to the true doctrines of Christ would be the salvation of Christianity and the world, for not only would mankind then worship Him in spirit and in truth, but they would put aside all hypocrisy and begin to love their neighbors as themselves.[99]

Let us move to something now that is sure to startle you a little. C.S. Lewis spoke of priestcraft and the apostate condition of general Christianity. Remember, this is from someone who belonged to the Church of England:

> When Catholicism goes bad it becomes the world-old, world-wide *religion* of amulets and holy places and priestcraft: Protestantism, in its corresponding decay, becomes a vague mist of ethical platitudes. Catholicism is accused of being much too like all the other religions; Protestantism of being insufficiently like a religion at all.[100]

In contrast to apostasy and priestcraft, he knew (or at least speculated) what people would be like if they lived by the true gospel of Jesus Christ (somewhere out there!). In the next excerpt he describes these people — these "new men" — that are alive in the Lord:

> Already the new men are dotted here and there all over the earth. Some, as I have admitted, are still hardly recognizable: but others can be recognised. Every now and then one meets them. Their very voices and faces are different from ours; stronger, quieter, happier, more radiant. They begin where most of us leave off. They are, I say, recognizable; but you must know what to look for. They will not be very like the idea of "religious people" which you have formed from your general reading. They do not draw attention to themselves. You tend to think that you are being kind to them when they are really being kind to you. They love you more than other men do, but they need you less. (We must get over wanting to be needed: in some goodish people, specially women, that is the hardest of all temptations to resist.) They will usually seem to have a lot of time: you will wonder where it comes from. When you have recognised one of them, you will recognise the next one much more easily. And I strongly suspect (but how should I know?) that they recognise one another immediately and infallibly, across every barrier of colour, sex, class, age, and even of creeds. In that way, to become holy is rather like joining a secret society. To put it at the very lowest, it must be great *fun*.[101]

How close can he get! I read this and think of our living prophets, apostles, and general authorities. These "new men" are so alive in Christ that they seem to almost radiate. They are powerful in the Spirit and strong in the truth. Also, his description of these special people sounds very much like how I have heard nonmembers describe "Mormons." "They have something special about them, some kind of a light or goodness — something hard to describe." Sound familiar? If only C.S.

Lewis could have met the Quorum of the Twelve — I think he would have found exactly what he was looking for. C.S. Lewis also said, "Men are mirrors, or 'carriers' of Christ to other men." *(Mere Christianity* p.148)

C.S. Lewis appreciated the doctrine of enduring to the end, and of continuous repentance. He knew that God would forgive us and work with us as long as we kept on honestly striving with real intent. He wrote:

> No *amount* of falls will really undo us if we keep on picking ourselves up each time. We shall of course be very muddy and tattered children by the time we reach home. But the bathrooms are all ready, the towels put out, and the clean clothes in the airing cupboard. The only fatal thing is to lose one's temper and give it up. It is when we notice the dirt that God is most present in us; it is the very sign of His presence.[102]

He also appreciated the importance of not getting so caught up in the means that we forget about the ends to be attained. We should keep focused on eternal life as our goal and strive for that. He wrote:

> He has substituted *religion* for God — as if navigation were substituted for arrival, or battle for victory, or wooing for marriage, or in general the means for the end. But even in this present life, there is danger in the very concept of *religion*. It carries the suggestion that this is one more department of life, an extra department added to the economic, the social, the intellectual, the recreational, and all the rest.[103]

Another principle to touch on is that of praying and having prayers answered. C.S. Lewis had a keen understanding of the truth, as we understand it, on this matter. Below is another excerpt from *The Screwtape Letters:*

> Don't forget to use the 'heads I win, tails you lose' argument. If the thing he prays for doesn't happen, then that is one more proof that petitionary prayers don't work; if it does happen, he will, of course, be able to see some of the physical causes which led up to it, and 'therefore it would have happened anyway', and thus a granted prayer becomes just as good a proof as a denied one that prayers are ineffective.[104]

Now consider the following ideas by C.S. Lewis regarding the tough job of perfection and pursuing joy. He wrote:

We are half-hearted creatures, fooling about with drink and sex and ambition when infinite joy is offered us, like an ignorant child who wants to go on making mud pies in a slum because he cannot imagine what is meant by the offer of a holiday at the sea…We are far too easily pleased. *(The Problem of Pain)*

Also:

I think that many of us, when Christ has enabled us to overcome one or two sins that were an obvious nuisance, are inclined to feel (though we do not put it into words) that we are now good enough. He has done all we wanted Him to do, and we should be obliged if He would now leave us alone. As we say "I never expected to be a saint, I only wanted to be a decent ordinary chap." And we imagine when we say this that we are being humble. Your bid — for God or no God, for a good God or the Cosmic Sadist, for eternal life or nonentity — will not be serious if nothing much is staked on it. And you will never discover how serious it was until the stakes are raised horribly high; until you find that you are playing not for counters or for sixpences but for every penny you have in the world.[105]

Yes, this mortality is very serious business, for so much is staked on it. That is why God keeps sending prophets and exhorts us to pray and read our scriptures, and on and on — because of the incredible importance of this tiny blip of our existence.

There are two minor concepts to hit before the conclusion — the Word of Wisdom and the phrase "clear as the moon, and fair as the sun, and terrible as an army with banners." First, the Word of Wisdom. C.S. Lewis once wrote, "…creatures like us who actually find hatred such a pleasure that to give it up is like giving up beer or tobacco…" He was illustrating a point about forgiveness and overcoming hatred, but at the same time touched upon an idea we call the Word of Wisdom. Next, point in the *Doctrine and Covenants*, the Lord said:

And to none else will I grant this power, to receive this same testimony among this generation, in this the beginning of the rising up and the coming forth of my church out of the wilderness — clear as the moon, and fair as the sun, and terrible as an army with banners.[106]

C.S. Lewis also used some of the same wording to describe the true church as he saw it. He said, "…the Church as we see her spread out though all time and space and rooted in eternity, terrible as an army with banners." The only place in the Bible that uses these same words is in Song of Solomon — just an interesting sidenote.

To conclude, *The Book of Mormon* teaches what the purpose of this life is, and the importance of our mortal probation. We read from Alma 12:24:

> And we see that death comes upon mankind, yea, the death which has been spoken of by Amulek, which is the temporal death; nevertheless there was a space granted unto man in which he might repent; therefore this life became a probationary state; a time to prepare to meet God; a time to prepare for that endless state which has been spoken of by us, which is after the resurrection of the dead.[107]

Now compare this with a very moving and powerfully written religious "pep talk" by C.S. Lewis:

> Why is God landing in this enemy-occupied world in disguise and starting a sort of secret society to undermine the devil? Why is He not landing in force, invading it? Is it that He is not strong enough? Well, Christians think He is going to land in force; we do not know when, but we can guess why He is delaying. He wants to give us the chance of joining His side freely. I do not suppose you and I would have thought much of a Frenchman who waited till the Allies were marching into Germany and then announced he was on our side. God will invade. But I wonder whether people who ask God to interfere openly and directly in our world quite realize what it will be like when He does. When that happens, it is the end of the world. When the author walks on to the stage the play is over. God is going to invade, all right: but what is the good of saying you are on His side then, when you see the whole natural universe melting away like a dream and something else — something it never entered your head to conceive — comes crashing in; something so beautiful to some of us and so terrible to others that none of us will have any choice left? For this time it will be God without disguise; something so overwhelming that it will strike either irresistible love or irresistible horror into every creature. It will be too late then to choose your side. There is no use saying you choose to lie down when it has become impossible to stand up. That will not be the time for choosing: it will be the time when we discover which side we really have chosen, whether we realized it before or not. Now, today, this moment, is our chance to choose the right side. God is holding back to give us that chance. It will not last for ever. We must take it or leave it.[108]

Quite motivational, isn't it? C.S. Lewis was very zealous and enthusiastic when it came to articulating the cause of truth, and what we are to be about down here on this earth. May we remember his words, and especially those of the apostle Paul to fight a good fight, to finish our course, and to keep the faith! [109]

> Yea, wo be unto him that
> hearkeneth unto the precepts of
> men, and denieth the power of
> God, and the gift of the Holy Ghost!
>
> — 2 Nephi 28:26

CHAPTER 7

The Philosophies of Men

Ideas tend to surface and float around in the world that undermine truth and circumvent fact. We often call these things the philosophies or precepts of men, especially when the false ideas come in the context of religion. These false philosophies are often the result of reasoning, logic, hear-say, even intentional fabrication, and the fruits of these seeds sometimes lead to shattered faith, warped morals, and watered-down principles. Elder Bruce R. McConkie commented on these philosophies of men in the following way:

> The wisdom of the world results from the uninspired reflections, research, and discoveries of men. It is composed of partial and fragmentary truths mixed with error. Theorizing and hypothecating commonly accompany it. This type of wisdom includes the philosophies and learning of men which are destructive of faith. Astrology, organic evolution, the so-called higher criticism which denies the divinity of Christ, and any supposed knowledge which rules God out of the picture, falls in this category.[110]

He includes organic evolution as one of those philosophies that "are destructive of faith," and so C.S. Lewis seemed to agree. He wrote the following about what he called "universal evolutionism:"

> By universal evolutionism I mean the belief that the very formula of universal process is from imperfect to perfect, from small beginnings to great endings, from the rudimentary to the elaborate: the belief which makes people find it natural to think that morality springs from savage taboos, adult sentiment from infantile sexual maladjustments, thought from instinct, mind from matter, organic from inorganic, cosmos from chaos. This is perhaps the deepest habit of mind in the contemporary world. It seems to

me immensely unplausible, because it makes the general course of nature so very unlike those parts of nature we can observe.[111]

Bruce R. McConkie wrote, "The philosophies of men find followers, while the revealed truths of the gospel are shunned."[112] C.S. Lewis calls the evolution philosophy "immensely unplausible," and it seems that what he is referring to — in different words — is this philosophy that perfection evolves independent of God. That perfection is the natural state of things, and all change is leading toward perfection. We know that perfection can only come about through the aid of our Heavenly Father, and that if left to themselves, things tend to decay away from perfection. We also know from *The Book of Mormon* that man in the natural state "is an enemy to God." (Mosiah 3:19)

C.S. Lewis held some contempt for the philosophies of men and the "wisdom" and reasoning of the world. He understood that falsehoods float around, especially in academic circles, and he didn't put much stock in the latest novelty of ideas presented by the intelligentsia. It is certain that the father of lies himself is directly or indirectly behind false doctrines, and C.S. Lewis knew that lies were often mingled with truth to make them more palatable and acceptable. He wrote in his book, *The Last Battle*, "And then she understood the devilish cunning of the enemies' plan. By mixing a little truth with it they had made their lie far stronger."[113]

One myth that has floated around a great deal lately (and indeed, also in C.S. Lewis' generation) is the psychological idea of getting things out in the open and looking at sin as more of a psychological phenomenon than of an evil thing that must be repented of. Elder Neal A. Maxwell once wrote:

> *The Book of Mormon* suggests a third reason why we may like complexity and reject simplicity, and that is because complexity is pleasing to the carnal mind. It gives us sanctuaries for sin.[114]

From Spencer W. Kimball we have, "...when toleration for sin increases, the outlook is bleak and Sodom and Gomorrah days are certain to return."[115] On this very idea, C.S. Lewis wrote the following wise and interesting commentary:

> We are told to "get things out into the open," not for the sake of self-humiliation, but on the ground that these "things" are very natural and we need not be ashamed of them. But unless Christianity is wholly false, the perception of ourselves which we

have in moments of shame must be the only true one; and even Pagan society has usually recognised "shamelessness" as the nadir of the soul. In trying to extirpate Shame we have broken down one of the ramparts of the human spirit, madly exulting in the work...It is mad work to remove hypocrisy by removing the temptation to hypocrisy: the "frankness" of people sunk below shame is a very cheap frankness.[116]

Perhaps shame is one of the warning alarms of our conscience (the light of Christ) telling us that something we have done is wrong, and needs correction. Modern psychology has sought to eradicate shame as an archaic and unnecessarily burdensome myth that might as well be thrown away. When people abandon shame and conscience, they soon become past feeling and engulfed in sin, for it is shame that turns the crank of our repentance. C.S. Lewis gave us the following about the doctrine of sin, and the importance of recognizing it for what it is:

A recovery of the old sense of sin is essential to Christianity...Most of us have at times felt a secret sympathy with the dying farmer who replied to the Vicar's dissertation on repentance by asking "What harm have I ever done *Him?*" There is the real nub.[117]

Another philosophy of men that has been around for a long, long time is that of Adam and Eve really botching things up in the Garden, and because of this, all of us must suffer for their sin. C.S. Lewis knew this was incorrect, and wrote accordingly. He said:

Our present condition, then, is explained by the fact that we are members of a spoiled species. I do not mean that our sufferings are a punishment for being what we cannot now help being nor that we are morally responsible for the rebellion of a remote ancestor.[118]

From the 2nd Article of Faith we have, "We believe that men will be punished for their own sins, and not for Adam's transgression."

There is another idea which does not draw its falseness from itself so much as from the sum of the parts of other true doctrines. I speak of the idea that says we can pick and choose the truths and doctrines we want to live by, and as for the ones we don't — well, those weren't really intended for us anyway. C.S. Lewis begs to differ. He wrote:

We have all departed from that total plan in different ways, and each of us wants to make out that his own modification of the original plan is the plan itself. You will find this again and again about anything that is really Christian: every one is attracted by bits of it and wants to pick out those bits and leave the rest. That is why we do not get much further: and that is why people who are fighting for quite opposite things can both say they are fighting for Christianity.[119]

He understood how important it was to accept the fullness of the gospel, although he didn't understand that term *per se* in the sense of the gospel being restored by Joseph Smith. But he did know that it was dangerous to glean those truths for ourselves that were comfortable and fit with our personal agenda. Five years before C.S. Lewis' death, Hugh B. Brown spoke the following in a general conference:

> We think neither individuals nor groups of men, under whatever title, are justified in their attempts to pick and choose between particular aspects of the whole gospel. We profoundly dissent from the opinion that there is an element in the message which changes with varying conditions. The message of the Church of Jesus Christ of Latter-day Saints is that there has been a restoration of the identical gospel which Jesus taught and which the apostles preached at his command. It is a gospel of glad tidings of great joy, a gospel of hope and saving power as was enjoyed by members of the Church in the days of the Savior and his apostles.[120]

Truly, we must not trifle with the gospel and pick the parts we like. We must square ourselves honestly with it, and live by it to the best of our ability.

Here is an interesting tidbit for you. C.S Lewis wrote once, "The second thing — the philosophy of Freud — is in direct contradiction to Christianity." Ezra Taft Benson said the following concerning Freud:

> As a watchman on the tower, I feel to warn you that one of the chief means of misleading our youth and destroying the family unit is our educational institutions. There is more than one reason why the Church is advising our youth to attend colleges close to their homes where institutes of religion are available. It gives the parents the opportunity to stay close to their children, and if they become alerted and informed, these parents can help expose some of the deceptions of men like Sigmund Freud, Charles Darwin, John Dewey, John Keynes, and others.[121]

The Lord's anointed are here to teach us truth and expose falsehoods. Another small point lies in President Benson's warning of our educational institutions. Compare that comment with one by C.S. Lewis:

> Almost our whole education has been directed to silencing this shy, persistent, inner voice; almost all our modern philosophies have been devised to convince us that the good of man is to be found on this earth.[122]

This quote is loaded with profound parallels of our beliefs. His "shy, persistent, inner voice" sounds like the Holy Ghost (i.e., the still small voice). He implies that the good of man is not to be found on this earth. Just as Jesus said that His kingdom is not of this world, we should not try to plant our hearts and happiness in this world.

Another important falsehood of which C.S. Lewis was well aware, consisted of the rampant and widespread indulgences in immorality. One of the main culprits behind this problem is the media, and it was the same in C.S. Lewis' time. He wrote:

> In the first place our warped natures, the devils who tempt us, and all the contemporary propaganda for lust, combine to make us feel that the desires we are resisting are so "natural," so "healthy," and so reasonable, that it is almost perverse and abnormal to resist them. Poster after poster, film after film, novel after novel, associate the idea of sexual indulgence with the ideas of health, normality, youth, frankness, and good humour. Now this association is a lie. Like all powerful lies, it is based on a truth — the truth, acknowledged above, that sex in itself (apart from the excesses and obsessions that have grown round it) is "normal" and "healthy," and all the rest of it. The lie consists in the suggestion that any sexual act to which you are tempted at the moment is also healthy and normal. Now this, on any conceivable view, and quite apart from Christianity, must be nonsense. Surrender to all our desires obviously leads to impotence, disease, jealousies, lies, concealment, and everything that is the reverse of health, good humour, and frankness. For any happiness, even in this world, quite a lot of restraint is going to be necessary; so the claim made by every desire, when it is strong, to be healthy and reasonable, counts for nothing. Every sane and civilized man must have some set of principles by which he chooses to reject some of his desires and to permit others.[123]

To concur with the above opinion, Ezra Taft Benson taught the following in 1986:

We counsel you, young men, not to pollute your minds with such degrading matter, for the mind through which this filth passes is never the same afterwards. Don't see R-rated movies or vulgar videos or participate in any entertainment that is immoral, suggestive, or pornographic. Don't listen to music that is degrading.[124]

Also, Bruce R. McConkie stated, "And all these iniquities receive anything but deterrence from the common run of movies, radio and television broadcasts, comic books, and other cheap and degrading so-called literary efforts."[125] C.S. Lewis' above quote is right on target when he says, "Every sane and civilized man must have some set of principles by which he chooses to reject some of his desires and to permit others." The hedonistic philosophy of doing whatever happens to feel good at any time produces animals, not saints. Self control has always been a fundamental aspect of true Christian living, not to mention abstaining from immoral behavior.

In the following excerpt, C.S. Lewis strikes upon two points. One is the old controversy over faith and works, and the other is the apostate doctrine of paying money to be forgiven of sins. Concerning faith and works — that is dealt with more fully in another chapter. We will discuss the second point here. First, from Mormon 8:32 we have, "Yea, it shall come in a day when there shall be churches built up that shall say: Come unto me, and for your money you shall be forgiven of your sins." How prophetic! C.S. Lewis wrote:

> There are two parodies of the truth which different sets of Christians have, in the past, been accused by other Christians of believing: perhaps they may make the truth clearer. One set were accused of saying, Good actions are all that matters. The best good action is charity. The best kind of charity is giving money. The best thing to give money to is the Church. So hand us over £10,000 and we will see you through." The answer to that nonsense, of course, would be that good actions done for that motive, done with the idea that Heaven can be bought, would not be good actions at all, but only commercial speculations. The other set were accused of saying, "Faith is all that matters. Consequently, if you have faith, it doesn't matter what you do. Sin away, my lad, and have a good time and Christ will see that it makes no difference in the end." The answer to that nonsense is that, if what you call your "faith" in Christ does not involve taking the slightest notice of what He says, then it is not Faith at all — not faith or trust in Him, but only intellectual acceptance of some theory about Him.[126]

Nephi prophesied:

And there shall also be many which shall say: Eat, drink, and be merry; nevertheless, fear God — he will justify in committing a little sin; yea, lie a little, take the advantage of one because of his words, dig a pit for thy neighbor; there is no harm in this; and do all these things, for tomorrow we die; and if it so be that we are guilty, God will beat us with a few stripes, and at last we shall be saved in the kingdom of God.[127]

C.S. Lewis understood, as we do, the inherent dangers in the philosophy of materialism. Note first the following excerpts about materialism from a few general authorities:

The unscrupulous Christians who have aggressively promoted the priorities of materialism and preyed upon the victims of that philosophy come within the prophet Isaiah's condemnation of the sinner who benefits by "the gain of oppressions."[128]

LeGrand Richards wrote:

While modern philosophy, which believes in nothing but what you can touch, is overspreading the Atlantic states, Joseph Smith is creating a spiritual system, combined also with morals and industry, that may change the destiny of the race... We certainly want some such prophet to start up, take a big hold of the public mind — and stop the torrent of materialism that is hurrying the world into infidelity, immorality, licentiousness and crime."[129]

In his book *The Screwtape Letters,* Screwtape writes:

Don't waste time trying to make him think that materialism is *true!* Make him think it is strong or stark or courageous — that it is the philosophy of the future. That's the sort of thing he cares about.[130]

This is insightful. How often do we think about things other than in terms of truth? Do we not often use as our standard in moral judgments benchmarks outside true and false, or good and evil?

Although the subject of pride is more fully dealt with in another chapter, we should here note a few interesting points about intellectual pride. 2 Timothy 3:7 speaks of people "Ever learning, and never able to come to the knowledge of the truth." Ezra Taft Benson taught the following:

Yes, it is intellectual pride that leads one to think he is self-sufficient in matters of mind and of spirit. Let us ever realize the difference that exists between a discoverer of the truth and the Lawgiver of all truth. The first is human; the other divine.[131]

Here is another partial letter from Uncle Screwtape to Nephew Wormwood from *The Screwtape Letters:*

> Only the learned read old books, and we have now so dealt with the learned that they are of all men the least likely to acquire wisdom by doing so.[132]

This quickly brings to mind the ever-so-familiar words of Nephi in *The Book of Mormon:*

> O that cunning plan of the evil one! O the vainness, and the frailties, and the foolishness of men! When they are learned they think they are wise, and they hearken not unto the counsel of God, for they set it aside, supposing they know of themselves, wherefore, their wisdom is foolishness and it profiteth them not. And they shall perish. (2 Nephi 9:28)

So many intellectuals are sucked into this clever trap — and C.S. Lewis knew it. Thankfully, we have a long history of prophets and many of their records in the scriptures. These messengers deliver for us timely truth from God, and are a striking and truthful contrast to the flood of propaganda continually rolling in from scholarly hypothesizing. Again on the subject of science we have an excerpt from *The Screwtape Letters.* It reads:

> If he must dabble in science, keep him on economics and soci- ology; don't let him get away from that invaluable "real life." But the best of all is to let him read no science but to give him a grand general idea that he knows it all and that everything he happens to have picked up in casual talk and reading is "the results of modern investigation." Do remember you are there to fuddle him. From the way some of you young fiends talk, anyone would suppose it was our job to teach![133]

C.S. Lewis had a friend who one night had a spiritual experience out in the desert. He believed he somehow felt or experienced God, and concluded from this that the only true religion is to be felt and enjoyed out in nature. He felt that this outdoor experience proved that "church" and doctrines, etc. were merely inventions of man. Of this experience, C.S. Lewis wrote the following:

> Merely learning and thinking about the Christian doctrines, if you stop there, is less real and less exciting than the sort of thing my friend got in the desert. Doctrines are not God: they are only a kind of map. But that map is based on the experience of hundreds of people who really were in touch with God — experience compared with which any thrills or pious feelings you and I are likely to get on our own are very elementary and very confused. And secondly, if you want to get any further, you must use the map. You see, what happened to the man in the desert may have been real, and was certainly exciting, but nothing comes of it. It leads nowhere. There is nothing to do about it. In fact, that is just why a vague religion — all about feeling God in nature, and so on — is so attractive. It is all thrills and no work; like watching the waves from the beach. But you will not get to Newfoundland by studying the Atlantic that way, and you will not get eternal life by simply feeling the presence of God in flowers or music. Neither will you get anywhere by looking at maps without going to sea. Nor will you be very safe if you go to sea without a map.[134]

It is easy for us to want to seek after an easy religion. In the example above, Nature provided an easy religion — one requiring no work or sacrifice. These easy religions have drawn flocks of followers, and it is no wonder why. The problem is, these simple, whipped-topping religions do not have the power to exalt. The religion whose God asked Abraham to sacrifice his son, and asked Lehi to take his family into the wilderness, was not an easy religion — just the true one.

Remember in the *Doctrine and Covenants* where the Lord exhorts his saints to beware of "evils and designs" in the last days? Here is the reference:

> Behold, verily, thus saith the Lord unto you: In consequence of evils and designs which do and will exist in the hearts of conspiring men in the last days, I have warned you, and forewarn you, by giving unto you this word of wisdom by revelation — (D&C 89:4)

C.S. Lewis somehow understood this principle, in a sense, and knew that there were conspiring men doing evil things. Compare the following excerpt from *The Screwtape Letters* with the above revelation from the Lord:

> In a rough-and-ready way, of course, this question is decided for us by spirits far deeper down in the Lowerarchy than you and I. It is the business of these great masters to produce in every age a general misdirection of what may be called sexual "taste." This

they do by working though the small circle of popular artists, dressmakers, actresses, and advertisers who determine the fashionable type. The aim is to guide each sex away from those members of the other with whom spiritually helpful, happy, and fertile marriages are most likely.[135]

While the Lord's revelation and this excerpt from C.S. Lewis are apparently speaking of different specific things, fundamentally, they are parallel with one another in a broader sense.

Now we should touch on, just for a moment, the idea that has come to be known as "the generation gap." Both Ezra Taft Benson and C.S. Lewis seemed to think alike on this one, though they didn't put in the same words. Ezra Taft Benson said in 1970:

> And so let's strengthen the family...In such homes there is no "generation gap." This deceptive phrase is another tool of the devil to weaken the home and family. Children who honor their parents and parents who love their children can make a home a haven of safety and a little bit of heaven.[136]

Compare this concept, now with the following from Uncle Screwtape the devil:

> To regard the ancient writer as a possible source of knowledge — to anticipate that what he said could possibly modify your thoughts or your behaviour — this would be reflected as unutterably simple-minded. And since we cannot deceive the whole human race all the time, it is most important thus to cut every generation off from all others; for where learning makes a free commerce between the ages there is always the danger that the characteristic errors of one may be corrected by the characteristic truths of another. But, thanks be to Our Father and the Historical Point of View, great scholars are now as little nourished by the past as the most ignorant mechanic who holds that "history is bunk."[137]

Satan could obviously use this "generation gap" idea to his advantage, as put so eloquently (and humorously) in the excerpt above. In an extension of the above idea, C.S. Lewis (via Screwtape) illustrates the point of how often things become "fashionable" that are contrary to truth and happiness. He writes:

> Thus we make it fashionable to expose the dangers of enthusiasm at the very moment when they are all really becoming worldly and lukewarm; a century later, when we are really making them all Byronic and drunk with emotion, the fashionable

outcry is directed against the dangers of the mere "understanding." Cruel ages are put on their guard against Sentimentality, feckless and idle ones against Respectability, lecherous ones against Puritanism; and whenever all men are really hastening to be slaves or tyrants we make Liberalism the prime bogey. *(The Screwtape Letters, pg.92-93)*

Another dangerous philosophy of men is that of interpreting the Bible far too loosely, and stretching "metaphorical" teachings into something watered down and far from the truth. C.S. Lewis wrote of this:

Some people when they say that a thing is meant 'metaphorically' conclude from this that it is hardly meant at all. They rightly think that Christ spoke metaphorically when he told us to carry the cross: they wrongly conclude that carrying the cross means nothing more than leading a respectable life and subscribing moderately to charities. They reasonably think that hell 'fire' is a metaphor — and unwisely conclude that it means nothing more serious than remorse. They say that the story of the Fall in Genesis is not literal; and then go on to say that it was really a fall upwards — which is like saying that because 'My heart is broken' contains a metaphor, it therefore means 'I feel very cheerful'. This mode of interpretation I regard, frankly, as nonsense. For me the Christian doctrines which are 'metaphorical' — or which have become metaphorical with the increase of abstract thought — mean something which is just as 'supernatural' or shocking after we have removed the ancient imagery as it was before.[138]

The above commentary is a much-needed perspective in today's world — perhaps much more so today than when the words were written. And speaking of interpreting scripture, here is a sidenote: C.S. Lewis said, "Odd, the way the less the Bible is read the more it is translated."[139]

Another philosophy or precept that the adversary seems to use successfully is that he convinces people that religion is only a crutch, or perhaps a phase which will soon pass. The following is a brilliant communique, again from Uncle Screwtape to his nephew, about helping people think that their interest in religion (actually the Holy Ghost working on them) is really just a phase. He writes:

Another possibility is that of direct attack on his faith...Can you not persuade him that "this religious phase" is just going to die away like all his previous phases? Of course, there is no conceivable way of getting by reason from the proposition "I am losing interest in this" to the proposition "This is false."

But, as I said before, it is jargon, not reason, you must rely on. The mere *word phase* will very likely do the trick. I assume that the creature has been through several of them before — they all have — and that he always feels superior and patronizing to the ones he has emerged from, not because he has really criticized them but simply because they are in the past. (You keep him well fed on hazy ideas of Progress and Development and the Historical Point of View, I trust, and give him lots of modern biographies to read? The people in them are always emerging from Phases, aren't they?)

You see the idea? Keep his mind off the plain antitheses between True and False. Nice shadowy expressions — "It was a phase" — "I've been through all that" — don't forget the blessed word "Adolescent." *(The Screwtape Letters, pg.45)*

How smooth and seductive and appetizing the above rationale is, and how easily we tend to fall into it.

In the world of educational philosophy, they teach to be very careful of accepting anything on authority, of believing something just because someone else has said so. This is logical and rational to a point, but creates grave dangers if extended into spiritual spheres. In this state of mind we begin questioning everything taken from authority, and suddenly we're questioning the prophets and God Himself. Fortunately, we have the Holy Ghost to give us our own personal witness of truths, but we must take on authority directions from the prophets. Consider the following from *Mere Christianity*, by C.S. Lewis, on the subject:

Do not be scared by the word authority. Believing things on authority only means believing them because you have been told them by someone you think trustworthy. Ninety-nine per cent of the things you believe are believed on authority. I believe there is such a place as New York. I have not seen it myself. I could not prove by abstract reasoning that there must be such a place, I believe it because reliable people have told me so. The ordinary man believes in the Solar System, atoms, evolution, and the circulation of the blood on authority — because the scientists say so. Every historical statement in the world is believed on authority. None of us has seen the Norman Conquest or the defeat of the Armada. None of us could prove then by pure logic as you prove a thing in mathematics. We believe them simply because people who did see them have left writings that tell us about them: in fact, on authority. A man who jibbed at authority in other things as some people do in religion would have to be content to know nothing all his life.[140]

That is where faith comes in. Something inside of us tells us that some truth we have heard or read is indeed true, yet we may have no "scientific" evidence of its truthfulness. No matter. We must be true to the light within.

Now let us observe a philosophy quite common to the psychiatric profession: that religion is nothing more than a placebo, a mental tool that helps people to cope with harsh realities. While Karl Marx would have agreed with this, C.S. Lewis strongly disagreed. He wrote:

> Keep clear of psychiatrists unless you know that they are also Christians. Otherwise they start with the assumption that your religion is an illusion and try to 'cure' it: and this assumption they make not as professional psychologists but as amateur philosophers. Often they have never given the question any serious thought.[141]

His brilliant usage of words is refreshing coming from one who was a strong defender of Christianity.

For the Spirit speaketh the truth
and lieth not.Wherefore, it speaketh
of things as they really are, and of
things as they really will be.

— Jacob 4:13

CHAPTER 8

The Truest Realist

Our society tends to admire realists, or at least to respect them. Realism, in its true sense, is a good thing. But I think the whole concept has been twisted and dirtied in some instances. Many people have come to think of a realist as someone who doesn't give in to all the phony religious nonsense, and simply trusts in what he can see, feel, prove, etc. C.S. Lewis had a remarkable perspective on the realist. He wrote, "[Christ] was the only man who never yielded to temptation...also the only man who knows to the full what temptation means — the only complete realist." *(Mere Christianity,* pg.110)

Many of our leaders and general authorities seem to agree with this concept. Observe what they had to say about the realist. First, from Elder Mark E. Petersen: "But to the true realist, God is a great and significant reality who guides the ultimate destiny of the world."[142] Truly, if a realist in the most definitional sense, is one who accepts and embraces what is real, then a belief in God is mandatory. An atheist, then, becomes a fantasist, or an escapist. Elder Neal A. Maxwell spoke of those who call themselves realists those who also sin and revel in it. He said:

> When those who call themselves realists urge us to yield to the temptations of the flesh, because everybody's doing it or because that's how things are, the living God (through the living prophets, Church, and scriptures) reminds us, not of how things seem to be, but of how things really are. The genuine realist is really able to "consider the lilies in the field" and thereby see a planning and a providing God in marvelous microcosm — or he can consider the heavens and see God moving in majestic and marvelous macrocosm! (D&C 84:82; 88:47)[143]

Perhaps the world's idea of a realist is quite contrary to what the gospel describes. God is truth, and therefore reality. On the other hand, Satan is the father of lies and deception, and therefore anti-reality. Interesting, isn't it? Mark E. Petersen taught, "To the true realist, God is a significant presence who guides the ultimate destiny of the world. But let us never forget that one of his most basic laws concerns morality."[144] Expounding further on this concept, Elder Maxwell also said:

> The true religionist is actually the ultimate realist, for he has a fully realistic view of man and the universe; he traffics in truths that are culminating and everlasting; he does not focus on facts that fade with changing circumstances or data that dissolve under pressures of time and circumstance. The Lord said, "...truth abideth and hath no end." (D&C 88:66) The ultimate realist also comes to know real liberty, for "where the Spirit of the Lord is, there is liberty" also. (2 Corinthians 3:17) When we go against God and things as they really are, as George MacDonald taught, the universe becomes our prison cell.[145]

Some critics of the gospel have said that Jesus was too much of an idealist, and not enough of a realist. Elder Paul H. Dunn taught the following in contrast to the above idea:

> If the fault is said to be in Jesus because he was too idealistic for this hardheaded, practical world, our witness is that Jesus was as much of a realist as an idealist — the real and ideal merge in his life and teachings. It is the world that has not been realistic and has not been able to take him at his word. He said that mankind is a brotherhood. The world has said that mankind ought to be a brotherhood. We have failed to take his realism seriously, and our problems multiply and grow in complexity.[146]

He is right when he says the world has not been realistic. Christ tries to draw us into the truth, and therefore become more realistic. Sin leads away from truth and from reality.

Elder Maxwell also spoke of the realist in terms of submissiveness, and of not hiding from truth. He taught:

> When we reflect upon our need for such submissiveness, it is not solely a matter of subordination. Submissiveness involves an invitation to come to grips with reality — to come into harmony with "things as they really are." Only then, proceeding from where one now is, can genuine spiritual progress be made. This is

not mysticism, but realism; the acceptance of the truth of things as they were, as they are, and as they will become, as God's purposes for individuals and mankind unfold in the universe. Refusing to look at these realities or shielding our eyes from them — these are signs of immaturity, whereas looking with wide-eyed wonder but with eyes of faith is an act of high intelligence.[147]

We must make ourselves right with Him or we can never enter into that reality which is eternal life.

And now abideth faith, hope,
charity, these three; but the
greatest of these (is) charity.

— 1 Corinthians 13:13

CHAPTER 9

Faith, Hope, and Charity

C.S. Lewis had quite an accurate and profound view of faith, hope, and charity, as we understand them. These three virtues are tantamount in *The Book of Mormon,* and perhaps one of the primary themes of the book. We know much more about faith, hope, and charity from *The Book of Mormon* than we could know from the Bible alone, and C.S. Lewis had a surprising understanding of these virtues, even based upon what is in *The Book of Mormon.*

FAITH

C.S. Lewis believed that faith, and our ability to choose, are spiritually related. He wrote:

> There must perhaps always be just enough lack of demonstrative certainty to make free choice possible; for what could we do but accept if the faith were like the multiplication table?[148]

This understanding of faith is essentially parallel to what Alma taught the Zoramites when he said:

> Yea, there are many who do say: If thou wilt show unto us a sign from heaven, then we shall know of a surety; then we shall believe.

> Now I ask, is this faith? Behold, I say unto you, Nay; for if a man knoweth a thing he hath no cause to believe, for he knoweth it. (Alma 32:17-18)

C.S. Lewis' "demonstrative certainty" is the same thing as Alma's "sign." Joseph Smith taught the school of the prophets in Kirtland the importance of faith as a principle of power, and a necessity for our sanctification. That is why God requires it of us, rather than just giving us a sure knowledge of everything immediately.

C.S. Lewis also spoke of faith relative to those who have lost their faith. He wrote:

> If you examined a hundred people who had lost their faith in Christianity, I wonder how many of them would turn out to have been reasoned out of it by honest argument? Do not most people simply drift away?[149]

How true this is! Christianity can neither be proved nor disproved in the customary scientific way — and that is so by design. Thus, the whole system is prepared that enables us to have faith, and to grow in that sanctifying principle.

HOPE

Hope is usually mentioned in the middle of our triad of virtues. We know that hope not only brings comfort, peace, and assurance, but it is also essential to salvation. Moroni taught, "...wherefore man must hope, or he cannot receive an inheritance in the place which thou has prepared." (Ether 12:32) C.S Lewis understood this doctrine to the letter. Consider the following brief, but brilliant comment on hope:

> Hope is one of the Theological virtues. This means that a continual looking forward to the eternal world is not (as some modern people think) a form of escapism or wishful thinking, but one of the things a Christian is meant to do.[150]

Hope, like faith, is a principle of power and sanctification. Despair is the opposite of hope, and Moroni taught that despair comes because of iniquity (Mor. 10:22). Therefore, hope is really the fruit of righteousness, just as despair is the fruit of iniquity.

CHARITY

Charity, or the pure love of Christ, is the capping, perfecting virtue on top of faith and hope. Paul in the Bible taught that without faith we are nothing, and Moroni in *The Book of Mormon* expounds on the specifics of charity. C.S Lewis understood the importance of charity, and even came strikingly close to it by our definition of "the pure love of Christ." He said, "Charity means love, in the Christian sense." (*Mere Christianity*, pg.100) He also associated charity with giving to the poor. He wrote:

Charity — giving to the poor — is an essential part of Christian morality: in the frightening parable of the sheep and the goats it seems to be the point on which everything turns. Some people nowadays say that charity ought to be unnecessary and that instead of giving to the poor we ought to be producing a society in which there were no poor to give to. They may be quite right in saying that we ought to produce that kind of society. But if anyone thinks that, as a consequence, you can stop giving in the meantime, then he has parted company with all Christian morality. I do not believe one can settle how much we ought to give. I am afraid the only safe rule is to give more than we can spare. In other words, if our expenditure on comforts, luxuries, amusements, etc, is up to the standard common among those with the same income as our own, we are probably giving away too little. If our charities do not at all pinch or hamper us, I should say they are too small. There ought to be things we should like to do and cannot do because our charitable expenditure excludes them. I am speaking now of "charities" in the common way. Particular cases of distress among your own relatives, friends, neighbors or employees, which God, as it were, forces upon your notice, may demand much more: even to the crippling and endangering of your own position. For many of us the great obstacles to charity lies not in our luxurious living or desire for more money, but in our fear — fear of insecurity.[151]

Compare his profound insights with those found in Mosiah 4 — perhaps one of the greatest sermons on giving to the poor in all scripture:

And now, if God, who has created you, on whom you are dependent for your lives and for all that ye have and are, doth grant unto you whatsoever ye ask that is right, in faith, believing that ye shall receive, O then, how ye ought to impart of the substance that ye have one to another.

And if ye judge the man who putteth up his petition to you for your substance that he perish not, and condemn him, how much more just will be your condemnation for withholding your substance, which doth not belong to you but to God, to whom also your life belongeth; and yet ye put up no petition, nor repent of the thing which thou hast done.

I say unto you, wo be unto that man, for his substance shall perish with him; and now, I say these things unto those who are rich as pertaining to the things of this world.

And now, for the sake of these things which I have spoken unto you — that is, for the sake of retaining a remission of your sins from day to day, that ye may walk guiltless before God — I would that ye should impart of your substance to the poor, every man according to that which he hath, such as feeding the hungry, clothing the naked, visiting the sick and administering to their relief, both spiritually and temporally, according to their wants.[152]

It becomes quickly apparent that C.S. Lewis has really tapped into a vein of truth in the matter of charity, and giving to the poor. I think this is because he sincerely sought for the truth, and took Jesus' words in the Bible to heart.

But I would have you know, that the head of every man is Christ; and the head of the woman [is] the man; and the head of Christ [is] God.

— 1 Corinthians 11:3

CHAPTER 10

An Unpopular Doctrine

One issue that has come to the front is that of sexual equality. Increasing numbers of women are entering the work force. Sexual discrimination and harassment in the work force have become prominent issues. More women are going to college, becoming professionals, and entering the political arena. With all of this has come different attitudes by women, and about women concerning the role of the woman, in the home. Historically, leadership in the home has been vested in the male, while the woman was expected to abide by her husband's counsel. Perhaps the roots of this philosophy rest somewhat in the teachings of the apostle Paul. He taught that "the head of the woman is the man." (1 Cor. 11:3) Doctrines in the Bible that speak of these sorts of unpopular principles have been largely ignored, and even contradicted. However, C.S. Lewis seemed to believe that there is something true and God-ordained about the man presiding in the home. He wrote:

> Something else, even more unpopular, remains to be dealt with. Christian wives promise to obey their husbands. In Christian marriage the man is said to be the "Head." Two questions obviously arise here. (1) Why should there be a head at all — why not equality? (2) Why should it be the man?
>
> (1) The need for some head follows from the idea that marriage is permanent. Of course, as long as the husband and wife are agreed, no question of a head need arise; and we may hope that this will be the normal state of affairs in a Christian marriage. But when there is a real disagreement, what is to happen? Talk it over, of course; but I am assuming they have done that and still failed to reach agreement. What do they do next? They cannot decide by a majority vote, for in a council of two there can be no majority. Surely, only one or

other of two things can happen: either they must separate and go their own ways or else one or other of them must have a casting vote. If marriage is permanent, one or other party must, in the last resort, have the power of deciding the family policy. You cannot have a permanent association without a constitution.

(2) If there must be a head, why the man? Well, firstly, is there any very serious wish that is should be the woman? As I have said, I am not married myself, but as far as I can see, even a woman who wants to be the head of their own house does not usually admire the same state of things when she finds it going on next door. She is much more likely to say "Poor Mr. X! Why he allows that appalling woman to boss him about the way she does is more than I can imagine." I do not think she is even very flattered if anyone mentions the fact of her own "headship." There must be something unnatural about the rule of wives over husbands, because the wives themselves are half ashamed of it and despise the husbands whom they rule. But there is also another reason; and here I speak quite frankly as a bachelor, because it is a reason you can see from outside even better than from inside. The relations of the family to the outer world — what might be called its foreign policy — must depend, in the last resort, upon the man, because he always ought to be, and usually is, much more just to the outsider. A woman is primarily fighting for her own children and husband against the rest of the world. Naturally, almost, in a sense, rightly, their claims override, for her all other claims. She is the special trustee for their interests. The function of the husband is to see that this natural preference of hers is not given its head. He has the last word in order to protect other people from the intense family patriotism of the wife. If anyone doubts this, let me ask a simple question. If your dog has bitten the child next door, or if your child has hurt the dog next door, which would you sooner have to deal with, the master of that house or the mistress? Or if you are a married woman, let me ask you this question. Much as you admire your husband, would you not say that his chief failing is his tendency not to stick up for his right and yours against the neighbors as vigorously as you would like? A bit of an Appeaser?[153]

This is quite a philosophy. There are many ideas presented above that deserve serious thought, however uncomfortable or unpopular (on the surface) his ideas may be. Our prophets have always taught that the husband and father should preside in the home, and this has been unpopular with a good many people also. Brigham Young taught this on the subject:

I exhort you, masters, fathers, and husbands, to be affectionate and kind to those you preside over. And let them be obedient, let the wife be subject to her husband, and the children to their parents. Mothers, let your minds be sanctified before the Lord, for this is the commencement, the true foundation of a proper education in your children, the beginning point to form a disposition in your offspring, that will bring honor, glory, comfort, and satisfaction to you all your lifetime.[154]

In the next excerpt, C.S. Lewis speaks on Christian obedience in general, as well as the previous principle. He then comments on the state of what we would call a Zion society. There are three examples in the scriptures of societies that actually attained Zion on earth, or at least came very close to it. These were the City of Enoch, the Nephite nation immediately following the coming of Christ, and the true Christians mentioned in the book of Acts, immediately following Christ's ascension. C.S. Lewis wrote the following concerning this type of Zion society:

[A Christian society] is always insisting on obedience — obedience (and outward marks of respect) from all of us to properly appointed magistrates, from children to parent, and (I am afraid this is going to be very unpopular) from wives to husbands. Thirdly, it is to be a cheerful society: full of singing and rejoicing, and regarding worry or anxiety as wrong.[155]

Compare his idea of the Christian society with a revelation from God to Brigham Young, recorded in the *Doctrine and Covenants*:

If thou art merry, praise the Lord with singing, with music, with dancing, and with a prayer of praise and thanksgiving. (D&C 136:28)

The Lord obviously approves and encourages singing, music, and (contrary to centuries of superstition) dancing. Bruce R. McConkie believed strongly in the divinity and beauty of music. He once wrote:

Music is part of the language of the Gods. It has been given to man so he can sing praises to the Lord. It is a means of expressing, with poetic words and in melodious tunes, the deep feelings of rejoicing and thanksgiving found in the hearts of those who have testimonies of the divine Sonship and who know of the wonders and glories wrought for them by the Father, Son, and Holy Spirit. Music is both in the voice and in the heart. Every true saint finds his heart full of songs of praise to his Maker. Those whose voices can sing forth the praises found in their hearts are twice blest. "Be filled with the Spirit," Paul counseled, "Speaking to yourselves in psalms and hymns and spiritual songs singing and making melody in your heart to the Lord." (Eph. 5:18-19) Also: "Let the word of Christ dwell in you richly in all wisdom; teaching and admonishing one another in psalms and hymns and spiritual songs, singing with grace in your hearts to the Lord." (Col. 3:16)[156]

Behold, here is the agency of man,
and here is the condemnation of man;
that which was from the beginning is
plainly manifest unto them, and they
receive not the light.

— D&C 93:31

CHAPTER 11

Agency

The primary dilemma confronted in C.S. Lewis' book *The Problem of Pain* is this: if God is powerful and good, why does He allow so much suffering and misery in the world? You will see in this chapter what an impressive grasp he has on this whole idea. Through the restored gospel of Jesus Christ, we have many answers and insights about the purpose of life, and why God permits suffering. Elder Neal A. Maxwell taught the following in regard to this:

> Embedded in the profound truths of the Restoration is relief from the painful dilemmas which have caused some to stumble and fall. Significant answers are now available to cruel questions such as "If God is good and omnipotent, why does He permit suffering and evil?" In response thereto we learn important truths about the combined consequences of misused agency and about the role of divine tutoring. Some challenges built into life are "common to all men." Infant mortality is not left as a dangling dilemma. And in the just plan of God there are provisions for those who do not hear the gospel in mortality. These and other answers underscore the ultimate justice and mercy of God.[157]

C.S. Lewis understood many of these things to an astonishing degree. First, concerning the age-old question of why God allows suffering, C.S. Lewis offers the following perspective:

> We can, perhaps, conceive of a world in which God corrected the results of this abuse of free will by His creatures at every moment: so that a wooden beam became soft as grass when it was used as a weapon, and the air refused to obey me if I attempted to set up in it the sound waves that carry lies or insults. But such a

world would be one in which wrong actions were impossible, and in which, therefore, freedom of the will would be void; nay, if the principle were carried out to its logical conclusion, evil thought would be impossible, for the cerebral matter which we use in thinking would refuse its task when we attempted to frame them. All matter in the neighborhood of wicked man would be liable to undergo unpredictable alterations. That God can and does, on occasions, modify the behaviour of matter and produce what we call miracles, is part of the Christian faith; but the very conception of a common, and therefore, stable, world, demands that these occasions should be extremely rare.[158]

This brings to mind Lucifer's pre-mortal plan to force good behavior. From the above analogy we can well see why this plan was rejected. When God granted unto mankind their agency, He created the possibility of joy and exaltation for each soul. But He also, in a manner of speaking, opened Pandora's box; for with agency comes the potential of profound righteousness and profound wickedness. You could say it comes with the territory. There is ultimate justice, however, on judgment day — as well as ultimate reward. Nephi the prophet expounded on the needs and effects of agency in the following manner:

> For it must needs be, that there is an opposition in all things. If not so, my first-born in the wilderness, righteousness could not be brought to pass, neither wickedness, neither holiness nor misery, neither good nor bad. Wherefore, all things must needs be a compound in one; wherefore, if it should be one body it must needs remain as dead, having no life neither death, nor corruption nor incorruption, happiness nor misery, neither sense nor insensibility. (2 Nephi 2:11)

This is a principle with many rough edges, because we have seen how easily wicked men have brought about the death and misery of many souls. But how could God consistently prevent evil without unravelling agency for all? Consider the following by Elder Neal A. Maxwell:

> If the Lord were to show His power as some expect power to be used — which is virtually unthinkable — mortals would experience, among other things, prompt punishment rather than divine long-suffering. God would then stop all human suffering and silence all opposition to His work. In countless ways He would control the adverse effects of agency merely to prove that He was all-powerful. But He would not be all-loving for in effect He would have derailed His plan of happiness! The enforced

cooperation would not produce illuminated individuality but an indistinguishable "compound in one." (2 Nephi 2:11) We would then be back to that proposal of enforced "salvation" rejected so long ago. (Moses 4:1)[159]

Notice the parallels between the above statement and the preceding one by C.S. Lewis. The Lord Himself said, "Woe unto the world because of offenses! for it must needs be that offenses come; but wo unto that man by whom the offense cometh!" (Matt. 18:3,7) God knew that offenses would come, for His plan of agency made these things possible. However, it is also apparent that just because God accounts for these offenses, He does not condone them — all things are done in wisdom and order.

In the midst of the doctrine of agency comes personal account-ability, and the fact that each person must sooner or later own up to his or her sins — either through repentance or final punishment. The Lord revealed the following principle to Joseph Smith regarding accountability:

That every man may act in doctrine and principle pertaining to futurity, according to the moral agency which I have given unto him, that every man may be accountable for his own sins in the day of judgment.[150]

Here is a related concept by C.S. Lewis:

...a world, thus continually underpropped and corrected by Divine interference, would have been a world in which nothing important ever depended on human choice, and in which choice itself would soon cease from the certainty that one of the apparent alternatives before you would lead to no results and was therefore not really an alternative.[161]

Again, from the *Doctrine and Covenants*:

Behold, here is the agency of man, and here is the condemna-tion of man; because that which was from the beginning is plainly manifest unto them, and they receive not the light. (D&C 93:31)

In God's plan of happiness for us, choice is of the utmost impor-tance. It is through our daily choices that mold our character and our destiny. It is through these choices that prove to ourselves, to God, and to our fellowman whether we are on the Lord's side or against Him. Choice is something that is wholly ours, and we do with our lives as we please. If we choose righteousness, we will be rewarded with the natural fruit of righteousness — happiness. If we choose wickedness we receive the natural fruit of the same — misery.

As has been mentioned before, free will creates the possibility of both righteousness and wickedness. We have potential exaltation on one hand and Pandora's Box on the other. Of this idea, C.S. Lewis wrote:

> If a thing is free to be good it is also free to be bad. And free will is what has made evil possible. Why, then, did God give them free will? Because free will, though it makes evil possible, is also the only thing that makes possible any love or goodness or joy worth having. A world of automata — of creatures that worked like machines — would hardly be worth creating. The happiness which God designs for His higher creatures is the happiness of being freely, voluntarily united to Him and to each other in an ecstasy of love and delight compared with which the most rapturous love between a man and a woman on this earth is mere milk and water. And for that they must be free.[162]

It is through choice and choice alone that all ultimately good and evil things come about. To do something really good or really awful for humanity we must thoroughly intend to do so. Jesus wrought out the infinite atonement through choice. It was premeditated, and He knew in advance that He would go through with it. Hitler also chose and meticulously planned the mass destruction he brought about.

Some may ask, with the tremendous potential of suffering and evil that agency creates, is agency even worth it? Is it a price worth paying? Think about what C.S. Lewis had to say on the matter in the next excerpt:

> If God thinks this state of war in the universe a price worth paying for free will — that is, for making a live world in which creatures can do real good or harm and something of real importance can happen, instead of a toy world which only moves when he pulls the strings — then we may take it it is worth paying.[163]

Our own wisdom can in no way compete with the wisdom of Him who created earth and heaven and gave mankind intelligence. Therefore, C.S. Lewis must be right. If God thought agency a risk worth taking, then we can rest assured agency is the best thing. Additional insights on suffering related to agency are found in the following words of Elder Maxwell:

In difficult moments as we witness needless human suffering, such perspective can and should comfort us, too. Nor need we be immobilized by human suffering. Ever since God gave "unto man his agency" (Moses 7:32), avoidable human misery has been largely caused by wrong choices and wrong behavior. Without gospel perspective, however, some cite human misery as a reason to doubt or to deny God. Failing to understand God's plan, some even imply their own moral superiority because, unlike God, they really "care" about human suffering![164]

Now consider the following by C.S. Lewis. He understood, as many of our church leaders have taught, that most suffering in life comes about because of the wickedness (directly or indirectly) of others. He wrote:

I have tried to show in a previous chapter that the possibility of pain is inherent in the very existence of a world where souls can meet. When souls become wicked they will certainly use this possibility to hurt one another; and this, perhaps, accounts for four-fifths of the suffering of men. It is men, not God, who have produced racks, whips, prisons, slavery, guns, bayonets, and bombs; it is by human avarice or human stupidity, not by the churlishness of nature, that we have poverty and overwork. But there remains, nonetheless, much suffering which cannot thus be traced to ourselves. Even if all suffering were man-made, we should like to know the reason for the enormous permission to torture their fellows which God gives to the worst of men.[165]

The Book of Mormon teaches that everyone will be rewarded or punished according to their deeds done in life. Alma taught this to his son. He said:

And now behold, is the meaning of the word restoration to take a thing of a natural state and place it in an unnatural state, or to place it in a state opposite to its nature?

O, my son, this is not the case; but the meaning of the word restoration is to bring back again evil for evil, or carnal for carnal, or devilish for devilish — good for that which is good; righteous for that which is righteous; just for that which is just; merciful for that which is merciful. (Alma 41:12-13)

C.S. Lewis wrote of the dilemma of man's poor use of agency, and the problems we encounter when we are angry with God over this. He wrote:

Of course God knew what would happen if they used their
freedom the wrong way: apparently He thought it worth the risk.
Perhaps we feel inclined to disagree with Him. But there is a difficulty about disagreeing with God. He is the source from which all
your reasoning power comes: you could not be right and He
wrong any more than a stream can rise higher than its own source.
When you are arguing against Him you are arguing against the
very power that makes you able to argue at all: it is like cutting off
the branch you are sitting on.[166]

Just as Heaven is a place prepared for the righteous, Hell is a place
prepared for the wicked. C.S. Lewis fathomed this well, and knew
that wicked souls must be punished or the whole plan would be frus-
trated. In our enlightened day we don't like to speak of punishing
criminals. No, we want to correct, reform, educate, etc. Consider the
following lengthy, but fascinating scenario presented by C.S. Lewis:

First, there is an objection, in many minds, to the idea of
retributive punishment as such. This has been partly dealt with in
a previous chapter. It was there maintained that all punishment
became unjust if the ideas of ill-desert and retribution were
removed from it; and a core of righteousness was discovered
within the vindictive passion itself, in the demand that the evil
man must not be left perfectly satisfied with his own evil, that it
must be made to appear to him what it rightly appears to others
— evil. I said that Pain plants the flag of truth within a rebel
fortress. We were then discussing pain which might still lead to
repentance. How if it does not — if no further conquest than the
planting of the flag ever takes place? Let us try to be honest with
ourselves. Picture to yourself a man who has risen to wealth or
power by a continued course of treachery and cruelty, by
exploiting for purely selfish ends the noble notions of his victims,
laughing the while at their simplicity; who, having thus attained
success, uses it for the gratification of lust and hatred and finally
parts with the last rag of honour among thieves by betraying his
own accomplices and jeering at their last moments of bewildered
disillusionment. Suppose further, that he does all this, not (as we
like to imagine) tormented by remorse or even misgiving, but
eating like a schoolboy and sleeping like a healthy infant — a jolly,
ruddy-cheeked man, without a care in the world, unshakably
confident to the very end that he alone has found the answer to
the riddle of life, that God and man are fools whom he has got the
better of, that his way of life is utterly successful, satisfactory,
unassailable. We must be careful at this point. The least indulgence of the passion for revenge is very deadly sin. Christian
charity counsels us to make every effort for the conversion of such

a man: to prefer his conversion, at the peril of our own lives, perhaps of our own souls, to his punishment; to prefer it infinitely. But that is not the question. Supposing he will not be converted, what destiny in the eternal world can you regard as proper for him? Can you really desire that such a man, remaining what he is (and he must be able to do that if he has free will) should be confirmed forever in his present happiness should continue, for all eternity, to be perfectly convinced that the laugh is on his side? And if you cannot regard this as tolerable, is it only your wickedness — only spite — that prevents you from doing so? Or do you find that conflict between Justice and Mercy, which has sometimes seemed to you such an outmoded piece of theology, now actually at work in your own mind, and feeling very much as if it came to you from above, not from below? You are moved, not by a desire for the wretched creature's pain as such, but a truly ethical demand that, soon or late, the right should be asserted, the flag planted in this horribly rebellious soul, even if no fuller and better conquest is to follow. In a sense, it is better for the creature itself, even if it never becomes good, that it should know itself a failure, a mistake. Even mercy can hardly wish to such a man his eternal, contented continuance in such ghastly illusion. Thomas Aquinas said of suffering, as Aristotle had said of shame, that it was a thing not good in itself, but a thing which might have a certain goodness in particular circumstances. That is to say, if evil is present, pain at recognition of the evil, being a kind of knowledge, is relatively good; for the alternative is that the soul should be ignorant of the evil, or ignorant that the evil is contrary to its nature," either of which, says the philosopher, "is manifestly bad." And I think, though we tremble, we agree. The demand that God should forgive such a man while he remains what he is, is based on a confusion between condoning and forgiving. To condone an evil is simply to ignore it, to treat it as if it were good. But forgiveness needs to be accepted as well as offered if it is to be complete: and a man who admits no guilt can accept no forgiveness. I have begun with the conception of Hell as a positive retributive punishment inflicted by God because that is the form in which the doctrine is most repellent, and I wished to tackle the strongest objection. But, of course, though Our Lord often speaks of Hell as a sentence inflicted by a tribunal, He also says elsewhere that the judgement consists in the very fact that men prefer darkness to light, and that not He, but His "word," judges men. We are therefore at liberty — since the two conceptions, in the long run, mean the same thing — to think of this bad man's perdition not as a sentence imposed on him but as the mere fact of being what he is. The characteristic of lost souls is "their rejection of everything that is not simply themselves." Our imaginary egoist has tried to turn everything he meets into a province or appendage of the self. The taste for the *other*, that is, the very capacity for enjoying good, is quenched in him except in so far as his body still draws him into some rudimentary contact with an outer world. Death removes this last contact. He has his wish — to live wholly in the self and to make the best of what he finds there. And what he finds there is Hell.[167]

Now compare the following scriptures with the above writing, "And, behold, there is a place prepared for them from the beginning, which place is hell." (D&C 29:38) Consider also:

And now, my son, all men that are in a state of nature, or I would say, in a carnal state, are in the gall of bitterness and in the bonds of iniquity; they are without God in the world, and they have gone contrary to the nature of God; therefore, they are in a state contrary to the nature of happiness. (Alma 41:11)

And I said unto them that it was a representation of that awful hell, which the angel said unto me was prepared for the wicked. (1 Nephi 15:29)

And there is a place prepared, yea, even that awful hell of which I have spoken, and the devil is the preparator of it; wherefore the final state of the souls of men is to dwell in the kingdom of God, or to be cast out because of that justice of which I have spoken. (1 Nephi 15:35)

Lehi taught that everything has its opposite, or else all things would be a "compound in one." Hell is the opposite of Heaven because the attributes of each are opposite and contrary to each other. Below is another profound, though fictional, account regarding agency from C.S. Lewis' classic *The Great Divorce*:

'I hardly know, Sir. What some people say on earth is that the final loss of one soul gives the lie to all the joy of those who are saved.'

'Ye see it does not.'

'I feel in a way that it ought to.'

'That sounds very merciful: but see what lurks behind it.'

'What?'

'The demand of the loveless and the self-imprisoned that they should be allowed to blackmail the universe: that till they consent to be happy (on their own terms) no one else shall taste joy: that theirs should be the final power; that Hell should be able to veto Heaven.'[168]

C.S. Lewis also appreciated the importance of our choices and decisions every day. He knew that our little choices here and now culminate into the sum of our existence later on. He wrote:

> Good and evil both increase at compound interest. That is why the little decisions you and I make every day are of such infinite importance. The smallest good act today is the capture of a strategic point from which a few months later, you may be able to go on to victories you never dreamed of. An apparently trivial indulgence in lust or anger today is the loss of a ridge or railway line or bridgehead from which the enemy may launch an attack otherwise impossible.[169]

This is a keen insight. Everything we do can have eternal consequences, and that is probably why King Benjamin taught:

> But this much I can tell you, that if ye do not watch yourselves, and your thoughts, and your words, and your deeds, and observe the commandments of God, and continue in the faith of what ye have heard concerning the coming of our Lord, even unto the end of your lives, ye must perish. And now, O man, remember, and perish not. (Mosiah 4:30)

Thus we see the importance of our agency, and the culmination of our thoughts, words, and deeds. Consider the following by C.S. Lewis concerning bringing our lives in harmony with God, and choosing the Lord's side. C.S. Lewis wrote:

> [God] will strike either irresistible love or irresistible horror into every creature. It will be too late then to choose your side. There is no use saying you choose to lie down when it has become impossible to stand up. That will not be the time for choosing: it will be the time when we discover which side we really have chosen, whether we realized it before or not. Now, today, this moment, is our chance to choose the right side.[170]

I think of the hymn:

> Who's on the Lord's side? Who?
>
> Now is the time to show;
>
> We ask it fearlessly;
>
> Who's on the Lord's side? Who?

This is a pep-talk and an admonition worth listening to. When the Lord comes again, the time for choosing will be over. Recall the parable of the Ten Virgins. The marriage feast came, and five were not ready. So it shall be with us.

Because agency grants us freedom of choice from moment to moment, it also allows us to direct our own ultimate destinies. And because of this, no one can be forced into heaven. How could it be any other way? Some simply do not choose heaven — it does not fit within the nature of their lives and desires. Consider this on the matter by C.S. Lewis:

> I would pay any price to be able to say truthfully "All will be saved." But my reason retorts, "Without their will, or with it?" If I say "Without their will" I at once perceive a contradiction; how can the supreme voluntary act of self-surrender be involuntary? If I say "With their will," my reason replies "How if they *will not* give in?"   Mercy, detached from Justice, grows unmerciful.[171]

Compare his words with those of Alma:

> …whosoever will come may come and partake of the waters of life freely; and whosoever will not come the same is not compelled to come; but in the last day it shall be restored unto him according to his deeds. (Alma 42:27)

And thus, it is all up to us. We have the choice of our thoughts, words, and actions for today, and we have the choice of our destiny over the long term. We may partake, as Alma said, of the waters of life freely, but we will not be compelled. If we use our agency for good, then we will be in the process of conforming our lives to the nature of happiness. Let us remember the words of the Lord to Joseph Smith in the *Doctrine and Covenants*: "For what doth it profit a man if a gift is bestowed upon him, and he receive not the gift? Behold, he rejoices not in that which is given unto him, neither rejoices in him who is the giver of the gift."[172]

> And the Gentiles are lifted up
> in the pride of their eyes,
> and have stumbled...
>
> — 2 Nephi 26:20

CHAPTER 12

Pride

In April General Conference of 1989, President Ezra Taft Benson delivered perhaps his most famous talk — Beware Of Pride. He delineated the evils and specifics of pride that most of us had never considered. In the talk, he quotes a statement from our Oxford Scholar, C.S. Lewis. Many years ago C.S. Lewis wrote *Mere Christianity* and titled one of the chapters *The Great Sin*. The subject was pride. Compare President Benson's talk with C.S.'s chapter and note the almost uncanny parallels. First, from President Benson:

"In the premortal council, it was pride that felled Lucifer, "a son of the morning."

From C.S. Lewis:

It was through Pride that the devil became the devil: Pride leads to every other vice: it is the complete anti-God state of mind.

President Benson:

Most of us think of pride as self-centeredness, conceit, boastfulness, arrogance, or haughtiness. All of these are elements of the sin, but the heart, or core, is still missing. The central feature of pride is enmity — enmity toward God and enmity toward our fellowmen. Enmity means "hatred toward, hostility to, or a state of opposition." It is the power by which Satan wishes to reign over us.

C.S. Lewis:

Pride always means enmity — it is enmity. And not only enmity between man and man, but enmity to God.

The Restored Gospel According to C.S. Lewis

President Benson:

Pride is essentially competitive in nature. We pit our will against God's. When we direct our pride toward God, it is in the spirit of "my will and not thine be done." As Paul said, they "seek their own, not the things which are Jesus Christ's." (Philip. 2:21) Our will in competition to God's will allows desires, appetites, and passions to go unbridled.

C.S. Lewis:

Each person's pride is in competition with everyone else's pride. It is because I wanted to be the big noise at the party that I am so annoyed at someone else being the big noise. Two of a trade never agree. Now what you want to get clear is that Pride is *essentially* competitive — is competitive by its very nature — while the other vices are competitive only, so to speak, by accident.

President Benson:

Our will in competition to God's will allows desires, appetites, and passions to go unbridled. The proud cannot accept the authority of God giving direction to their lives. They pit their perceptions of truth against God's great knowledge, their abilities versus God's priesthood power, their accomplishments against His might works.

Our enmity toward God takes on many labels, such as rebellion, hardheartedness, stiff-neckedness, unrepentant, puffed up, easily offended, and sign seekers. The proud wish God would agree with them. They aren't interested in changing their opinions to agree with God's.

C.S. Lewis:

In God you come up against something which is in every respect immeasurably superior to yourself. Unless you know God as that — and, therefore, know yourself as nothing in comparison — you do not know God at all. As long as you are proud you cannot know God. A proud man is always looking down on things and people: and, of course, as long as you are looking down, you cannot see something that is above you.

President Benson:

Another major portion of this very prevalent sin of pride is enmity toward our fellowmen. We are tempted daily to elevate ourselves above others and diminish them.

The proud make every man their adversary by pitting their intellects, opinions, words, wealth, talents, or any other worldly measuring device against others. In the words of C.S. Lewis: "Pride gets no pleasure out of having something, only out of having more of it than the next man...It is the comparison that makes you proud: the pleasure of being above the rest. Once the element of competition has gone, pride has gone."

Some prideful people are not so concerned as to whether their wages meet their needs as they are that their wages are more than someone else's. Their reward is being a cut above the rest. This is the enmity of pride.

C.S. Lewis:

Pride gets no pleasure out of having something, only out of having more of it than the next man. We say that people are proud of being rich, or clever, or good-looking, but they are not. They are proud of being richer, or cleverer, or better-looking than others. If everyone else became equally rich, or clever, or good-looking there would be nothing to be proud about. It is the comparison that makes your proud: the pleasure of being above the rest. Once the element of competition has gone, pride has gone. That is why I say that Pride is essentially competitive in a way the other vices are not.

President Benson:

The proud love "the praise of men more than the praise of God." Our motives for the things we do are where the sin is manifest. Jesus said He did "always those things" that pleased God. Would we not do well to have the pleasing of God as our motive rather than to try to elevate ourselves above our brother and outdo another?

C.S. Lewis:

To love and admire anything outside yourself is to take one step away from utter spiritual ruin; though we shall not be well so long as we love and admire anything more than we love and admire God.

President Benson:

When Pride has a hold on our hearts, we lose our independence of the world and deliver our freedoms to the bondage of men's judgment. The world shouts louder than the whisperings of the Holy Ghost. The reasoning of men overrides the revelations of God, and the proud let go of the iron rod.

C.S. Lewis:

For Pride is spiritual cancer: it eats up the very possibility of love, or contentment, or even common sense.

President Benson:

Pride is a sin that can readily be seen in others but is rarely admitted in ourselves.

C.S. Lewis:

There is one vice of which no man in the world is free; which every one in the world loathes when he sees it in someone else; and of which hardly any people except Christians ever imagine that they are guilty themselves...There is no fault which makes a man more unpopular, and no fault which we are more uncon-scious of in ourselves. And the more we have it ourselves, the more we dislike it in others...The vice I am talking of is Pride...

President Benson:

Contention ranges from a hostile spoken word to worldwide conflicts. The scriptures tell us that "only by pride cometh contention." (Prov. 13:10)

C.S. Lewis:

What is it that makes a political leader or a whole nation go on and on, demanding more and more? Pride again.

President Benson:

Pride is the universal sin, the great vice. Yes, pride is the universal sin, the great vice. The antidote for pride is humility — meekness, submissiveness...Pride is the great stumbling block to Zion. I repeat: Pride is the great stumbling block to Zion.

C.S. Lewis:

> The essential vice, the utmost evil, is Pride…the virtue oppo-
> site to [pride], in Christian morals, is called Humility.

This comparison makes obvious the keen insights C.S. Lewis had on pride: what causes it, and what can end it. Take a look at what other modern apostles have said about this great vice. Elder Bruce R. McConkie said:

> Boasting in the arm of flesh, one of the commonest of all sins among worldly people, is a gross evil; it is a sin born of pride, a sin that creates a frame of mind which keeps men from turning to the Lord and accepting his saving grace. When a man engages in self exultation because of his riches, his political power, his worldly learning, his physical prowess, his business acumen, or even his works of righteousness, he is not in tune with the Spirit of the Lord. Salvation itself comes by the grace of God, "Not of works," that is not of the performances and outward display of the law, "lest any man should boast." (Eph. 2:4-22; Rom. 3:27) As King Benjamin asked, after explaining the goodness of God and the comparative nothingness of men, "Of what have ye to boast?" (Mosiah 2: 17-26)[173]

And from Elder Dallin Oaks:

> The second type of pride that is condemned in the scriptures is what I have chosen to call the pride of comparison. Like the appropriate pride of self-respect, it follows on our concluding that we have done well in competition. But unlike the pride of self-respect, the competition is not with some outside standard, like a four-minute mile or an errorless performance of a difficult task. The pride of comparison is the mental attitude that comes from competing with persons and concluding that we are "better" than they. This is the kind of pride Elder L. Tom Perry condemned: "Those who are more prosperous can become filled with pride, and they look down on their brothers and sisters who have less, thinking them inferior" ("United in Building the Kingdom of God," *Ensign*, May 1987, p. 33).[174]

To emphasize his views on competition, and how very few mortals are immune to it, C.S. Lewis wrote, "'To be' *means* 'to be in competition.'"[175] He further elaborated on pride when he wrote:

> The pleasure of pride is like the pleasure of scratching. If there is an itch one does want to scratch; but it is much nicer to have neither the itch nor the scratch. As long as we have the itch of self-

regard we shall want the pleasure of self-approval; but the happiest moments are those when we forget our precious selves and have neither but have everything else (God, our fellow humans, animals, the garden and the sky) instead.[176]

True enough, we tend to set ourselves up for pride; to create that environment in ourselves in which pride can flourish. And when he says, "the happiest moments are those when we forget our precious selves," he has hit upon a simple reality of life in that we clear our souls and create a happiness in which joy can exist. Joy and pride can not cohabitate peacefully. Recall the story of Lucifer. He wanted to be the preeminent One at all costs. He threw away heaven and God and all current or potential happiness that he might have received in his attempt to be Number One. Consider the following commentary by C.S. Lewis on pride from *The Problem of Pain*.

> From the moment a creature becomes aware of God as God and of itself as self, the terrible alternative of choosing God or self for the centre is opened to it. This sin is committed daily by young children and ignorant peasants as well as by sophisticated persons, by solitaires no less than by those who live in society: it is the fall in every individual life, and in each day of each individual life, the basic sin behind all particular sins: at this very moment you and I are either committing it, or about to commit it, or repenting it. We try, when we wake, to lay the new day at God's feet; before we have finished shaving, it becomes our day and God's share in it is felt as a tribute which we must pay out of "our own" pocket, a deduction from the time which ought, we feel, to be "our own." (*The Problem of Pain*, pg.75)

That is an insight worth noting, and perhaps, when you boil it right down, the essence of our test here in mortality. That test is to find out whether we will put our own selves first and foremost, or whether we will extend, put God first, and our neighbor, and so, make true happiness a possibility. Without this, there is no joy, there is only our trapped individuality which we have fought so hard to preserve.

C.S. Lewis knew that pride was really the sin behind all other sins. He knew that willful disobedience to God requires first an element of pride. When the Lord did not accept Cain's offering, Cain was angry and rebelled; this would not have happened, indeed could not have happened, had Cain been in a state of humility. When we say "My will be done, and not thine," we are asserting something terrible that can only end in misery if not corrected.

C.S. Lewis also knew that humility was the great counterpart and destroyer of pride, just as President Benson affirmed that humility is the antidote of pride. Although Jesus had all knowledge and power, He was and is the great Exemplar of humility. While others used their power to reign, Jesus served; while others used their power to destroy, Jesus healed. But the crucial thing, really, was that Jesus was always subject to the will of the Father and never departed from that humble obedience.

Eye hath not seen, nor ear heard,
neither have entered into the heart
of man, the things which God hath
prepared for them that love him.

— Corinthians 2:9

CHAPTER 13

Heaven and Godhood

"Most people," said C.S. Lewis, "if they had really learned to look into their own hearts, would know that they do want, and want acutely, something that cannot be had in this world."[177] We all long for something this world doesn't have to offer. Yet so often we try to find happiness in the world — in what the world has to offer. Elder Neal A. Maxwell offers an interesting observation on this dilemma. He said:

> What Satan put into the heads of our remote ancestors was the idea that they could `be like gods' — could set up on their own as if they had created themselves — be their own masters — invent some sort of happiness for themselves outside God, apart from God. And out of that hopeless attempt has come nearly all that we call human history — money, poverty, ambition, war, prostitution, classes, empires, slavery — the long terrible story of man trying to find something other than God which will make him happy.[178]

This commentary is philosophically provocative. Why should the human race look for things that won't satisfy eternally? Jesus counseled us not to lay up treasures on earth that rust, get stolen, break, and don't satisfy. He commanded us to lay up treasure in heaven. But what does this mean?

From Moses 1:39 we learn that God's work and glory is to bring about the immortality and eternal life of us — His children. Jesus admonished us to be perfect as He is perfect, and as Our Heavenly Father is perfect. But it is through the Restoration and the Prophet Joseph Smith that we know more expressly what this means. We are to become gods and enjoy eternal life in the same manner in which God now does. But, as everybody knows, we as a church are criticized extensively for our belief in the potential exaltation of men and women. We are really the only church on earth that believes we can become (through the grace of Christ) gods and goddesses. Despite this fact, C.S. Lewis believed in the doctrine as we do — and he was a member of the Church of England. How is it that he understood (and openly wrote of) this principle believed by the Latter-day Saints, but openly rebutted by the rest of the world?

Consider the following excerpt from his written work *A Grief Observed:*

> To make an organism which is also a spirit; to make that terrible oxymoron, a 'spiritual animal.' To take a poor primate, a beast with nerve-endings all over it, a creature with a stomach that wants to be filled, a breeding animal that wants its mate, and say, 'now get on with it. Become a god.'[179]

He knew what the destiny of mankind could be, if we were obedient to the Lord. He understood that heaven is much more than playing harps and singing hymns, as medieval Christianity has evolved that idea. Spencer W. Kimball taught also the destiny of man when he said:

> Man is the masterpiece — in all the creations of God nothing even approaches him. The animals were given instincts. They can seize food, escape from enemies, hide from danger, sleep and rest, but they have practically none of the faculties given to this god-man, to this god in embryo.[180]

C.S. Lewis also comprehended that the only way to heaven and eternal happiness is through the Lord's plan. There is no remedial course, no side road or shortcut, and no loophole. We must either embrace the gospel, ultimately, or settle for less than a fullness of joy. C.S. Lewis wrote:

> God gives what He has, not what He has not: He gives the happiness that there is, not the happiness that is not. To be God — to be like God and to share His goodness in creaturely response — to be miserable — these are the only three alternatives. If we will not learn to eat the only food that the universe grows — the only food that any possible universe ever can grow — then we must starve eternally.[181]

With his words in mind, consider a teaching by Lorenzo Snow on the same idea:

Our great purpose in life is to do the Father's will. We came into the world for a great purpose, the same as Jesus, our elder brother, to do the will and works of our Father. In this there is peace, joy and happiness, an increase of wisdom, knowledge, and the Power of God; outside of this are no promised blessings. Thus let us devote ourselves to righteousness, help each and all to be better and happier; do good to all and evil to none; honor God and obey His Priesthood; cultivate and preserve an enlightened conscience and follow the Holy Spirit; faint not, hold fast to what is good, endure to the end, and your cup of joy shall be full even to overflowing, for great shall be your reward for your trials and your sufferings under temptations, your fiery ordeals, your heart yearnings and tears; yea, our God will give you a crown of unfading glory, and make you kings and queens in the midst of your posterity, to rule in righteousness through the countless ages of eternities.[182]

In C.S. Lewis' day, as in ours, the whole concept of heaven was often set up as a target for ridicule. The materialists and atheists have an easy time of this because heaven cannot be observed in a test tube, experimented upon, seen, or touched. Of this difficulty C.S. Lewis wrote:

We are very shy nowadays of even mentioning heaven. We are afraid of the jeer about "pie in the sky," and of being told that we are trying to "escape" from the duty of making a happy world here and now into dreams of a happy world elsewhere. But either there is "pie in the sky" or there is not. If there is not, then Christianity is false, for this doctrine is woven into its whole fabric. If there is, then this truth, like any other, must be faced, whether it is useful at political meetings or not.[183]

Yes, C.S. Lewis was well aware of the destiny of man — of our potential to exaltation. He understood that Heaven is a good deal more than is understood by worldwide Christianity. He also understood, as Lehi did after his "Tree of Life" dream, that the world is full of those that would point the finger of scorn at people following God and pursuing eternal life. He knew that we must carry on in spite of this. Most of all, he knew that the gospel of Jesus Christ was true, and that it was the only way.

Yea, they are grasped with death, and hell; and death, and hell, and the devil, and all that have been seized therewith must stand before the throne of God, and be judged according to their works, from whence they must go into the place prepared for them, even a lake of fire and brimstone, which is endless torment.

— 2 Nephi 28:23

CHAPTER 14

Hell, Death, and the Devil

This chapter is not intended to be dark or negative, and I hope it does not come across as such. You may wonder why I have even included it in the book. The reason is that the doctrines mentioned in the title are so misunderstood in general Christianity, that when a man such as C.S. Lewis comes along with such a startlingly clear and true perspective on these things, it is worth some attention. Through Joseph Smith, the Restoration, and *The Book of Mormon*, we know a thousand times more than the rest of the world about hell, death, and the devil. But somehow, C.S. Lewis has come to understand on his own, or should I say, through the help of the Spirit, many of the truths we take for granted. Consider the following, for starters, on the nature of hell:

> 'Hell is a state of mind — ye never said a truer word. And every state of mind, left to itself, every shutting up of the creature within the dungeon of its own mind — is, in the end, Hell. But Heaven is not a state of mind. Heaven is reality itself. All that is fully real is Heavenly.'[184]

The imagery in scripture of fire, brimstone, and ascending flames must be metaphorical and symbolic, and he knew it. Hell is indeed a state of mind. When people casually speak of something on earth being "hell" they may be literally accurate. Hell can exist anywhere, as well can heaven.

Most Christians, if they believe in Hell at all, have a certain reluctance to talk about it as something real and inevitable for the wicked. C.S. Lewis said:

> They [the doctrines about hell] are not really removable from the teaching of Christ or of His Church. If we do not believe them our presence in this church is great tomfoolery. If we do, we must sometime overcome our spiritual prudery and mention them.[185]

Perhaps hell is often loathe to be mentioned from enlightened pulpits these days because ministers do not want to use scare tactics on their congregations. Or, perhaps because of the memory of the old days when hellfire and damnation was preached constantly to the agony of the flock. C.S. Lewis touched on the issue in this way:

> Servile fear is, to be sure, the lowest form of religion. But a god such that there could never be occasion for even servile fear, a safe god, a tame god, soon proclaims himself to any sound mind as a fantasy. I have met no people who fully disbelieved in Hell and also had a living and life-giving belief in Heaven.[186]

Usually if either concept of heaven or hell is rejected in a person's mind, the other one goes right along with it. The doctrines come in pairs — like sin and repentance.

On the subject of the devil, C.S. Lewis said, "Christians, then, believe that an evil power has made himself for the present the Prince of the World. And, of course, that raises problems." These "problems" are elaborated on by James E. Talmage in *Jesus the Christ*. He wrote:

> After the passing of those terrible times, and thence onward for a period of unspecified duration, Satan would deceive the world through false doctrines, spread by evil men masquerading as ministers of God, who would continue to cry "Lo, here is Christ; or, lo, he is there;" but against all such the Twelve were put on their guard, and through them and other teachers, whom they would call and ordain, would the world be warned. Deceiving prophets, emissaries of the devil, would be active, some alluring people into the deserts, and impelling them to hermit lives of pernicious asceticism, others insisting that Christ could be found in the secret chambers of monastic seclusion; and some of them showing forth through the power of Satan, such signs and wonders as "to seduce,

if it were possible, even the elect;" but of all such scheming of the prince of evil, the Lord admonished His own: "Believe it not;" and added, "take ye heed; behold I have foretold you all things."[187]

If an enemy is to be guarded against, the enemy must be identified. From all the mention of Satan in scripture, it seems that God believes it essential for us to recognise our foe, that we may defend ourselves against this unseen enemy. It is through this enemy that false doctrines begin, persecutions are initiated, and wars are conceived. C.S. Lewis provides a possible explanation of this enemy, his nature, and how he went wrong. He said:

> How did the Dark Power go wrong? Here, no doubt, we ask a question to which human beings cannot give an answer with any certainty. A reasonable (and traditional) guess, based on our own experiences of going wrong, can, however, be offered. The moment you have a self at all, there is a possibility of putting yourself first — wanting to be the centre — wanting to be God, in fact. That was the sin of Satan: and that was the sin he taught the human race. Some people think the fall of man had something to do with sex, but that is a mistake…What Satan put into the heads of our remote ancestors was the idea that they could "be like gods" — could set up on their own as if they had happiness for themselves outside God, apart form God. And out of that hopeless attempt has come nearly all that we call human history — money, poverty, ambition, war, prostitution, classes, empires, slavery — the long terrible story of man trying to find something other than God which will make him happy.[188]

We have from Isaiah 14:13 the following account:

> For thou hast said in thine heart, I will ascend into heaven, I will exalt my throne above the stars of God: I will sit also upon the mount of the congregation, in the sides of the north.

The adversary rebelled against God because of his pride and lust for power. Isaiah tells us he wanted to exalt his throne above the stars of God. When that proved impossible, he waged war against God Himself, and was thrust down to earth. Thus, we have evil in the world.

C.S. Lewis made the following comparison of heaven and hell. He wrote:

> We know much more about heaven than hell, for heaven is the home of humanity and therefore contains all that is implied in a glorified human life: but hell was not made for men. It is in no

sense parallel to heaven: it is "the darkness outside," the outer rim where being fades away into nonentity.[189]

C.S. Lewis makes an interesting point when he says "hell was not made for men." This may be true in the sense that universally, only God truly creates. And God only creates things that are good. Therefore, hell is simply the cold outside — the nothing — the absence of that which is good and beautiful. Contemplate the following by C.S. Lewis in relation to this:

> 'The whole difficulty of understanding Hell is that the thing to be understood is so nearly Nothing…it begins with a grumbling mood, and yourself still distinct from it: perhaps criticizing it. And yourself, in a dark hour, may will that mood, embrace it. You can repent and come out of it again. But there may come a day when you can do that no longer. Then there will be no you left to criticize the mood, nor even to enjoy it, but just the grumble itself going on forever like a machine.'[190]

Now consider the following words of the prophet Mormon regarding hell in relation to God. He taught:

> Behold, I say unto you that ye would be more miserable to dwell with a holy and just God, under a consciousness of your filthiness before him, than ye would to dwell with the damned souls in hell. (Mormon 9:4)

This perhaps illustrates the truth that hell isn't so much a place that we are thrown into, as it is somewhere we voluntarily (though unhappily) go into. Think of this in relation to the next excerpt by C.S. Lewis:

> I willingly believe that the damned are, in one sense, successful, rebels to the end; that the doors of hell are locked on the inside. I do not mean that the ghosts may not wish to come out of hell, in the vague fashion wherein an envious man "wishes" to be happy; but they certainly do not will even the first preliminary stages of that self-abandonment through which alone the soul can reach any good. They enjoy forever the horrible freedom they have demanded, and are therefore self-enslaved just as the blessed, forever submitting to obedience, become through all eternity more and more free.[191]

Compare the above with another from C.S. Lewis' classic *The Great Divorce:*

'There are only two kinds of people in the end: those who say to God, "Thy will be done," and those to whom God says, in the end, "Thy will be done." All that are in Hell choose it. Without that self-choice there could be no Hell. No soul that seriously and constantly desires joy will ever miss it.'[192]

When Satan's plan was rejected, I can only assume that if he had humbly submitted to the Father, all would have been fine. But no, Lucifer had to rebel, and in so doing threw himself out of heaven and into spiritual death. Mortals are faced with the same choice. Some, however, are dismayed and perplexed by the whole idea of hell. They believe it to be unfair and cruel. C.S. Lewis had this to say about it:

In the long run the answer to all those who object to the doctrine of hell is itself a question: "What are you asking God to do?" To wipe out their past sins and, at all costs, to give them a fresh start, smoothing every difficulty and offering every miraculous help? But He has done so, on Calvary. To forgive them? They will not be forgiven. To leave them alone? Alas, I am afraid that is what He does.[193]

As C.S. Lewis says, God simply leaves them alone because they want nothing to do with Him (even in this God grants their request!). Misery is the natural outgrowth of this choice — it cannot be avoided. In fact, we learn from the book of Moses that God and His angels weep because of the suffering of the wicked. Recall the account:

But behold, their sins shall be upon the heads of their fathers; Satan shall be their father, and misery shall be their doom; and the whole heavens shall weep over them, even all the workmanship of mine hands; wherefore should not the heavens weep, seeing these shall suffer?[194]

C.S. Lewis had another insight relative to the idea of people in heaven weeping. He said, "...there may be something not all unlike pains in heaven..."(*The Problem of Pain*, pg.152) It is tragic, yet in no way unjust, that the wicked suffer. God extends his love, mercy, and help "all the day long" for all people, yet some knowingly reject it all to pursue their own desires.

He believed also that hell was something that came when service and charity ceased. He wrote:

What is outside the system of self-giving is not earth, nor nature, nor "ordinary life," but simply and solely Hell. Yet even Hell derives from this law such reality as it has. That fierce imprisonment in the self is but the obverse of the self-giving which is absolute reality; the negative shape which the outer darkness takes by surrounding and defining the shape of the real, or which the real imposes on the darkness by having a shape and positive nature of its own.[195]

His idea of the "fierce imprisonment in the self" is a logical implication stemming from the denial of self-giving and charity. Paul taught that we are nothing if we have not charity. The reason God is in a state of a fullness of joy is because he constantly seeks to bless all of mankind. Indeed, His work and glory is to bring to pass the immortality and eternal life of man. The reason Satan is miserable is because he cares about no one but himself, and thus cuts himself off from all possible joy and from God Himself.

Consider the following important concept in *The Book of Mormon* taught by Alma about the relationship between hardening the heart and becoming prey to the devil:

And they that will harden their hearts, to them is given the lesser portion of the word until they know nothing concerning his mysteries; and then they are taken captive by the devil, and led by his will down to destruction. Now this is what is meant by the chains of hell. (Alma 12:11)

Now compare this with the following similar and thought-provoking idea by C.S. Lewis:

Remember that, as I said, the right direction leads not only to peace but to knowledge. When a man is getting better he understands more and more clearly the evil that is still left in him. when a man is getting worse, he understands his own badness less and less. A moderately bad man knows he is not very good: a thoroughly bad man thinks he is all right. This is common sense, really. You understand sleep when you are awake, not while you are sleeping. You can see mistakes in arithmetic when your mind is working properly: while you are making them you cannot see them. You can understand the nature of drunkenness when you are sober, not when you are drunk. Good people know about both good and evil: bad people do not know about either.[196]

I once read part of the journal of an early apostate of the church. While he was an apostle, his writing in the journal was clear, eloquent, and he exhibited insightful testimony. He wrote very little after his apostasy, but what was written was poor, dark, negative, and somewhat lacking in common sense.

C.S. Lewis ventured some writing also on how the devil became the devil, based on what is found in the Bible. He takes this idea and adds his own perspective as follows:

> The proper question is whether I believe in devils. I do. That is to say, I believe in angels, and I believe that some of these, by the abuse of their free will, have become enemies to God and, as a corollary, to us. These we may call devils. They do not differ in nature from good angels, but their nature is depraved. Devil is the opposite of angel only as Bad Man is the opposite of Good Man. Satan, the leader or dictator of devils, is the opposite, not of God, but of Michael.[197]

Compare this, now, with revealed truth about Lucifer from the prophet Nephi:

> And I, Lehi, according to the things which I have read, must needs suppose that an angel of God, according to that which is written, had fallen from heaven; wherefore, he became a devil, having sought that which was evil before God. (2 Nephi 2:17)

There is a lesson here. The fact that Lucifer fell obviously implies that he once was good. He did not come into existence as an evil creature, but became so through the use of his agency. Even though he was a prominent, good, and righteous leader before his fall, this could not save him when he chose to rebel against the giver of life and light. Outside of Him there was only darkness and corruption. Speaking of the character attributes of fallen beings, C.S Lewis said:

> Whatever else we attribute to beings who sinned through pride, we must not attribute this. Satan...fell through force of gravity. We must picture Hell as a state where everyone is perpetually concerned about his own dignity and advancement, where everyone has a grievance, and where everyone lives the deadly serious passions of envy, self-importance, and resentment.[198]

Unfortunately, these attributes are also very much a part of the world in which we live, and vie for our attention and adoption. Bruce R. McConkie spoke of this in saying:

> Similarly in many ecclesiastical, educational, and governmental circles today it is with some considerable pride that

holders of worldly titles are so addressed as to give pointed notice of the titled person's "superior" or at least distinctive status. In churches of Christendom there is aversion to receiving the deference attached to ministerial titles. These titles of honor are sought, and men who should rank themselves as brethren, vie for that pre-eminence presumed to attach to holders of them. But in the true Church, which is the brotherhood of Christ, worldly titles have a hollow ring. Our Lord's true ministers prefer to be greeted by the saints as brethren in the Lord rather than to glory in the honors of men.[199]

Think of this principle and compare the following prophecy with the above thoughts of C.S. Lewis and Bruce R. McConkie:

> And when these things have passed away a speedy destruction cometh unto my people; for, notwithstanding the pains of my soul, I have seen it; wherefore, I know that it shall come to pass; and they sell themselves for naught; for, for the reward of their pride and their foolishness they shall reap destruction; for because they yield unto the devil and choose works of darkness rather than light, therefore they must go down to hell. (2 Nephi 26:10)

There is a principle in the universe that says that darkness does not comprehend light; low intelligence does not comprehend high intelligence; animals do not comprehend man; man does not fully comprehend God, and those engulfed in sin do not comprehend righteousness. In C.S. Lewis' profound yet humorous book *The Screwtape Letters,* Screwtape is writing advice to his nephew Wormwood, and he hits upon this very concept, from the point of view of Hell. He writes:

> Members of His faction have frequently admitted that if ever we came to understand what He means by Love, the war would be over and we should reenter Heaven. And there lies the great task. We know that He cannot really love: nobody can; it doesn't make sense. If we could only find out what He is really up to! Hypothesis after hypothesis has been tried, and still we can't find out.[200]

The Lord told Joseph Smith:

> Behold, I am Jesus Christ, the Son of God. I am the same that came unto mine own, and mine own received me not. I am the light which shineth in darkness, and the darkness comprehendeth it not. (D&C 6:21)

And here is a similar excerpt from Screwtape, again from *The Screwtape Letters:*

> ...the greatest curse upon us is the failure of our Intelligence Department. If we could only find out what He is really up to! Alas, alas, that knowledge, in itself so hateful and mawkish a thing, should yet be necessary for Power! Sometimes I am almost in despair. All that sustains me is the conviction that our Realism, our rejection (in the face of all temptations) of all silly nonsense and claptrap, must win in the end.[201]

And once more from the *Doctrine and Covenants:*

> For verily I say unto you that I am Alpha and Omega, the beginning and the end, the light and the life of the world — a light that shineth in darkness and the darkness comprehendeth it not.[202]

Now observe another interesting excerpt from *The Screwtape Letters:*

> And all the time the joke is that the word "mine" in its fully possessive sense cannot be uttered by a human being about anything. In the long run either Our Father or the Enemy will say "mine" of each thing that exists, and specially of each man. They will find out in the end, never fear, to whom their time, their souls, and their bodies really belong — certainly not to them, whatever happens. At present the Enemy says "mine" of everything on the pedantic, legalistic ground that He made it. Our Father hopes in the end to say "mine" of all things on the more realistic and dynamic ground of conquest.[203]

Brigham Young and C.S. Lewis shared a common belief: that there is no music in hell. Brigham said:

> There is no music in hell, for all good music belongs to heaven. Sweet harmonious sounds give exquisite joy to human beings capable of appreciating music. I delight in hearing harmonious tones made by the human voice, by musical instruments, and by both combined. Every sweet musical sound that can be made belongs to the Saints and is for the Saints. Every flower, shrub and tree to beautify, and to gratify the taste and smell, and every sensation that gives to man joy and felicity are for the Saints who receive them from the Most High.[204]

If music is truly a good, beautiful, heavenly thing, then it only follows that there would be no music in hell. Compare Brigham

Young's statement above with the following by C.S. Lewis (again, from *The Screwtape Letters):*

> Music and silence — how I detest them both! How thankful we should be that ever since our Father entered Hell — though longer ago than humans, reckoning in light years, could express — no square inch of infernal space and no moment of infernal time has been surrendered to either of those abominable forces, but all has been occupied by Noise — Noise, the grand dynamism, the audible expression of all that is exultant, ruthless, and virile — Noise which alone defends us from silly qualms, despairing scruples, and impossible desires. We will make the whole universe a noise in the end. We have already made great strides in this direction as regarding the Earth. The melodies and silences of Heaven will be shouted down in the end.[205]

C.S. Lewis shared the same idea as Brigham Young, but took it one step farther — there is no silence in hell, either. The Lord in scripture frequently describes the activity of hell as weeping, wailing, and gnashing of teeth. This awful commotion would leave little room for music or silence.

L.D.S. doctrine is immersed in the truth that the universe is at war. When Satan rebelled against God and led away a third of the host of heaven, war had commenced. This war that began in the premortal life has continued full swing on earth, and we mortals are caught in the midst of it — and so it was meant to be. For it was necessary, we learn from *The Book of Mormon,* that we should be enticed by good and evil, thus giving us the choice of what side we will take. From Moses we have the following record:

> Wherefore, because that Satan rebelled against me, and sought to destroy the agency of man, which I, the Lord God, had given him, and also, that I should give unto him mine own power; by the power of mine Only Begotten, I caused that he should be cast down; (Moses 4:3)

Compare this with C.S. Lewis' words:

> One of the things that surprised me when I first read the New Testament seriously was that it talked so much about a Dark Power in the universe — a mighty evil spirit who was held to be the Power behind death and disease, and sin. The difference is that Christianity thinks this Dark Power was created by God, and was good when he was created, and went wrong. Christianity

agrees with Dualism that this universe is at war. But it does not think this is a war between independent power. It thinks it is a civil war, a rebellion, and that we are living in a part of the universe occupied by the rebel.[206]

In the next excerpt, C.S. Lewis explores the nature of people approaching heaven, and those approaching hell. He writes:

> You will remember that in the parable, the saved go to a place prepared for them, while the damned go to a place never made for men at all. To enter heaven is to become more human than you ever succeeded in being in earth; to enter hell is to be banished from humanity. What is "remains." To be a complete man means to have the passions obedient to the will and the will offered to God: to have been a man — to be an ex-man or "damned ghost" — would presumably mean to consist of a will utterly centered in its self and passions utterly uncontrolled by the will. It is, of course, impossible to imagine what the consciousness of such a creature — already a loose congeries of mutually antagonistic sins rather than a sinner — would be like. *(The Problem of Pain, pg.125 & 126)*

In the next two excerpts, C.S. Lewis reveals his insight into the idea of individual choices leading us to our destiny — whether it be heaven or hell.

> Be sure there is something inside you which, unless it is altered, will put it out of God's power to prevent your being eternally miserable. While that something remains there can be no Heaven for you, just as there can be no sweet smells for a man with a cold in the nose, and no music for a man who is deaf. It's not a question of God 'sending' us to Hell. In each of us there is something growing up which will of itself be Hell unless it is nipped in the bud. The matter is serious: let us put ourselves in His hands at once — this very day, this hour.[207]

And:

> "There is always something they insist on keeping, even at the price of misery. There is always something they prefer to joy — that is, to reality."[208]

If we would just take that leap of faith and let go, then we would really be progressing to that joy that never ends. But we will all have to let go, sooner or later, of those things that bind us down and separate us from our Heavenly Father.

Now to conclude, C.S. Lewis illustrates the rewards and consequences of our perspective on life — on what we hold important and what we must sacrifice for heaven:

> If we insist on keeping Hell (or even earth) we shall not see Heaven: if we accept Heaven we shall not be able to retain even the smallest and most intimate souvenirs of Hell. I believe, to be sure, that any man who reaches Heaven will find that what he abandoned (even in plucking out his right eye) was precisely nothing: that the kernel of what he was really seeking even in his most depraved wishes will be there, beyond expectation, waiting for him in 'the High Countries'....
>
> I think earth, if chosen instead of heaven, will turn out to have been, all along, only a region in Hell: and earth, if put second to Heaven, to have been from the beginning a part of Heaven itself.[209]

"Husbands, love your wives, even
as Christ also loved the church,
and gave himself for it;"

— Ephesians 5:25

CHAPTER 14

Love and Marriage

Love and marriage are important parts of the restored gospel of Jesus Christ — especially with its emphasis on the eternal family. The Lord directed, "Thou shalt love thy wife with all thy heart, and shall cleave unto her and none else." (D&C 42:22) C.S. Lewis had several profound and insightful ideas regarding these principles. For example, Christian marriages all over the world, within the nuptial vows, include some provision about the marriage ending at death; but in our stories, music, and natural inclinations, we think of marriages lasting forever. Why this contradiction? C.S. Lewis said this of the matter:

...those who are in love have a natural inclination to bind themselves by promises. Love songs all over the world are full of vows of eternal constancy. The Christian law is not forcing upon the passion of love something which is foreign to that passion's own nature: it is demanding that loves should take seriously something which their passion of itself impels them to do.[210]

He also wrote:

It is simply no good trying to keep any thrill: that is the very worst thing you can do. Let the thrill go — let it die away — go on through that period of death into the quieter interest and happiness that follow — and you will find you are living in a world of new thrills all the time. But if you decide to make thrills your regular diet and try to prolong them artificially, they will all get weaker and weaker, and fewer and fewer, and you will be a bored, disillusioned old man for the rest of your life. It is because so few people understand this that you find many middle-aged men and women maundering about their lost youth, at the very age when new horizons ought to be appearing and new doors opening all round them. It is much better fun to learn to swim than to go on endlessly (and hopelessly) trying to get back the feeling you had when you first went paddling as a small boy. Knowledge can last, principles can last, habits can last; but feelings come and go. And in fact, whatever people say, the state called "being in love" usually does not last. If the old fairy-tale ending "They lived happily ever after" is taken to mean "The felt for the next fifty years exactly as they felt the day before they were married," then it says what probably never was nor ever could be true, and would be highly undesirable if it were. Who could bear to live in that excitement for even five years? What would become of your work, your appetite, your sleep, your friendships? But, of course, ceasing to be "in love" need not mean ceasing to love. Love in this second sense — love as distinct from 'begin in love" is not merely a feeling. It is a deep unity, maintained by the will and deliberately strengthened by habit;…They can have this love for each other even at those moments when they do not like each other;…"Being in love" first moved them to promise fidelity: this quieter love enables them to keep the promise. It is on this love that the engine of marriage is run: being in love was the explosion that started it.

If you disagree with me, of course, you will say, "He knows nothing about, he is not married." You may quite possibly be right. But before you say that, make quite sure that you are judging me by what you really know from your own experience and from watching the lives of your friends, and not by ideas you have derived from novels and films. This is not so easy to do as people think. Our experience is colored thorough and through by books and plays and cinemas, and it takes patience and skill to disentangle the things we have really learned from for ourselves.[211]

What a commentary on true love: the quiet, enduring, sacrificing, selfless love that sustains eternal marriages. In contrast to this, the following excerpt by C.S. Lewis expounds on the false and disillusioning concepts of marriage that are so prevalent. He wrote:

People get from books the idea that if you have married the right person you may expect to go on "being in love" for ever. As a result, when they find they are not, they think this proves they have made a mistake and are entitled to a change — not realizing that, when they have changed, the glamour will presently go out of the new love just as it went out of the old one. In this department of life, as in every other, thrills come at the beginning and do not last.[212]

C.S. Lewis has wise counsel and perspectives on the delicate art of marriage. His wisdom is worth considering, even though it runs counter to the prevailing portrayals of love in the media and elsewhere. He understood that sacrifice is just as essential for a long-term marriage as romance. Is it any coincidence that couples are married at an altar — the age-old symbol of sacrifice?

And behold, others he flattereth away, and telleth them there is no hell; and he saith unto them: I am no devil, for there is none — and thus he whispereth in their ears, until he grasps them with his awful chains, from whence there is no deliverance.

— Nephi 28:21-22

CHAPTER 16

Red Tights and Horns

I have often wondered how the devil has come to be depicted as a guy wearing red tights and having horns. Right now, today, Satan is depicted as something of a cartoon. The image is usually used in a humorous context. We see him in cartoons, television shows, and movies as a laughable (though wicked) person who is given as much credible reality by the creators of the cartoons as Peter Pan or Batman. Consider the following humorous yet insightful excerpt from *The Screwtape Letters* by C.S. Lewis. Uncle Screwtape is writing one of many letters to his nephew Wormwood, about how to tempt his human "patient" most effectively:

My dear Wormwood, I wonder you should ask me whether it is essential to keep the patient in ignorance of your own existence. That question, at least for the present phase of the struggle, has been answered for us by the High Command. Our policy, for the moment, is to conceal ourselves. Of course this has not always been so. We are really faced with a cruel dilemma. When the humans disbelieve in our existence we lose all the pleasing results of direct terrorism, and we make no magicians. On the other hand, when they believe in us, we cannot make them materialists and skeptics. At least, not yet. I have great hopes that we shall learn in due time how to emotionalise and mythologise their science to such an extent that what is in effect, a belief in us (though not under that name) will creep in while the human mind remains closed to belief in the Enemy. The "Life Force," the worship of sex, and some aspects of Psychoanalysis may here prove useful. If once we can produce our perfect work — the Materialist Magician, the man, not using, but veritably worshipping, what he vaguely calls "Forces" while denying the existence of "spirits" — then the end for the war will be in sight. But in the meantime we must obey our orders. I do not think you will have much difficulty in keeping the patient in the dark. The fact that "devils" are predominantly comic figures in the modern imagination will help you. If any faint suspicion of your existence begins to arise in his mind, suggest to him a picture of something in red tights, and persuade him that since he cannot believe in *that* (it is an old textbook method of confusing them) he therefore cannot believe in you.[213]

Given the present view of the devil, it would seem that the above "letter" contains more truth than fiction. The adversary's wholesale deception of modern man in this area rolls forward almost unimpeded. This myth the western world has adopted — a goofy and practically harmless image in red tights and horns — has proven a clever bluff with the power of steering millions away from the acute reality of the existence of the enemy of all righteousness. But what makes it all so insidious is the fact that when the devil is portrayed in this mythical and ridiculous manner, it is usually in the context of a very humorous situation. It's just a joke.

The inherent danger to us in our mortal probation is if people can be persuaded that Satan is fake or of the past, like Medusa or Achilles; then they not only put off their guard to temptation, but also begin to think of God as a similar relic or myth. Here is an interesting excerpt from Hugh Nibley on the matter:

> There is a precedent for the bit of faking — a most distinguished one. Satan, being neither stupid nor inexperienced, knows the value of a pleasing appearance — there are times when it pays to appear even as an angel of light. He goes farther than that, however, to assure that success of his masquerade (given out since the days of Adam) as a picturesquely repulsive figure — a four-star horror with claws, horns, or other obvious trimmings. With that idea firmly established, he can operate with devastating effectiveness as a very proper gentleman, a handsome and persuasive salesman. He "decoys" our minds (a favorite word with Brigham Young) with false words and appearances.[214]

Ezra Taft Benson spoke thus:

> Satan is a personal being. In these days of sophistication and error men depersonalize not only God but the devil. Under this concept Satan is a myth, useful for keeping people straight in less

enlightened days but outmoded in our educated age. Nothing is further from reality. Satan is very much a personal, individual spirit being, but without a mortal body. His desires to seal each of us his are no less ardent in wickedness than our Father's are in righteousness to attract us to his own eternal kingdom.[215]

This idea is all around us — from education to entertainment. Our society is slowly mutating "good" and "evil" into "useful" and "undesirable." Life is complicated, they say. Life is not black and white but all shades of complex grays. Thus it is not surprising, if we can't believe in a "good" and "evil" with hard edges and all, how can we believe in God and the devil? *The Book of Mormon* offers the straight and unsugared truth about what is happening:

> And behold, others he flattereth away, and telleth them there is no hell; and he saith unto them: I am no devil, for there is none — and thus he whispereth in their ears, until he grasps them with his awful chains, from whence there is no deliverance. (2 Nephi 28:21-22)

There is the danger! When Satan can convince someone that "I am no devil, for there is none" then he can grasp them with his "awful chains, from whence there is no deliverance." When our enemy is identified, there can be a battle, and we can defend ourselves. But, when the enemy walks around our camp unmolested, and we even refuse to acknowledge that he's there, danger is imminent. Think about the following from C.S. Lewis:

> I know someone will ask me, "Do you really mean, at this time of day, to re-introduce our old friend the devil — hoofs and horns and all?" Well, what the time of day has to do with it I do not know. And I am not particular about the hoofs and horns. But in other respects my answer is "Yes, I do." I do not claim to know anything about his personal appearance. If anybody really wants to know him better I would say to that person, "Don't worry. If you really want to, you will. Whether you'll like it when you do is another question."[216]

Not only has the devil been mythologized, but angels as well. Modern societies have come to think of them as Raphael's angels. C.S. Lewis wrote:

> It should be (but it is not) unnecessary to add that a belief in angels, whether good or evil, does not mean a belief in either as

they are represented in art and literature. Devils are depicted with bats' wings and good angels with birds' wings, not because anyone holds that moral deterioration would be likely to turn feathers into membrane, but because most men like birds better than bats. They are given wings at all in order to suggest the swiftness of unimpeded intellectual energy. They are given human form because man is the only rational creature we know. Creatures higher in the natural order than ourselves, either incorporeal or animated bodies of a sort we cannot experience, must be represented symbolically if they are to be represented at all.[217]

After being exposed to the culminated beliefs of centuries of apostasy, and independent of the Restored Gospel of Jesus Christ, could we have arrived at the same clear conclusions? Especially since the Bible metaphorically, but specifically, describes angels as having wings. But why the metaphor in the first place? Why wings? The best answer probably lies in the 77th section of the *Doctrine and Covenants*:

Q. What are we to understand by the eyes and wings, which the beasts had?

A. Their eyes are a representation of light and knowledge, that is, they are full of knowledge; and their wings are a representation of power, to move, to act, etc. (D&C 77:4)

This explanation of beasts could probably be ascribed to angels as well. In fact, Joseph Smith taught that angels don't have wings. The Bible is full of symbolism because often times symbols offer the most real description. Perhaps wings were attributed to angels simply because they are not bound down to the earth and subjected to the laws of gravity in the same sense that mortals are.

And the Spirit giveth light to every
man that cometh into the world;
and the Spirit enlighteneth every
man through the world, that
heakeneth to the voice of the Spirit.

— D&C 84:46

CHAPTER 17

Natural Law, Morality, and Relativism

Philosophers and statesmen have forever argued about how
people ought to act. Or, put another way, what sort of laws and
morals ought we adhere to and enforce? And, to what foundation or
standard should we build our laws from? This is where the idea of
Natural Law comes in. The Natural Law is sometimes thought of as
those set of principles derived from Nature itself, or from God. Our
Founding Fathers relied on these principles greatly in forming the
inspired Constitution. However, the precepts of men over the ages
have distorted the laws of God or invented their own entirely. These
variations from truth have sifted down through the ages and
become a part of many governments, societies, and ways of
thinking. The point in all this is to set the stage for C.S. Lewis' ideas
on Natural Law and morality. Compare his ideas with the truths we
have from the gospel:

Morality, like numinous awe, is a jump; in it, man goes beyond
anything that can be "given" in the facts of experience. And it has
one characteristic too remarkable to be ignored. The moralities
accepted among men may differ — though not, at bottom, so
widely as is often claimed — but they all agree in prescribing a
behavior which their adherents fail to practise. All men alike
stand condemned, not by alien codes of ethics, but by their own,
and all men therefore are conscious of guilt. The second element
in religion is the consciousness not merely of a moral law, but of a
moral law at once approved and disobeyed. This consciousness is
neither a logical, nor an illogical, inference from the facts of experience; if we did not bring it to our experience we could not find
it there. This is either inexplicable illusion, or else revelation.[218]

It is interesting that C.S. Lewis should mention the word revelation in connection with our conscience and the idea of natural law — implying, I think, the light of Christ. We know that this light of Christ is our conscience, or at least influences our conscience to a great extent. Revelation is light and truth from God to us, His children. While many have denied revelation, C.S. Lewis includes it as a basic part of religion and humanity. Take the following, for example, from his work *Miracles:*

> If we are to continue to make moral judgments (and whatever we say we shall in fact continue) then we must believe that the conscience of man is not a product of Nature. It can be valid only if it is an offshoot of some absolute moral wisdom, a moral wisdom which exists absolutely 'on its own' and is not a product of non-moral, non-rational Nature.[219]

Now from Bruce R. McConkie and the L.D.S. standpoint:

> Every person born into the world is endowed with the light of Christ (Spirit of Christ or of the Lord) as a free gift. (D&C 84:45-48) By virtue of this endowment all men automatically and intuitively know right from wrong and are encouraged and enticed to do what is right. (Mor. 7:16) The recognizable operation of this Spirit in enlightening the mind and striving to lead men to do right is called conscience. It is an inborn consciousness or sense of the moral goodness or blameworthiness of one's conduct, intentions, and character, together with an instinctive feeling or obligation to do right or be good.[220]

This instinctive, inborn desire to do what is right, in the form of the light of Christ, is really the only thing that (initially) enables us to recognize evil, and to choose good from evil. With Satan walking to and fro in the earth trying to lead us astray, we would certainly not be able to identify his evil without the counterbalancing effect of the light of Christ. Think about the following excerpt from *Mere Christianity* by C.S. Lewis. He points out our inborn knowledge of good versus evil, along with our difficulty in choosing the right:

> I hope you will not misunderstand what I am going to say. I am not preaching, and Heaven knows I do not pretend to be better than anyone else. I am only trying to call attention to a fact; the fact that this year, or this month, or, more likely, this very day, we have failed to practise ourselves the kind of behaviour we expect from other people. There may be all sorts of excuses for us.

That time you were so unfair to the children was when you were very tired. That slightly shady business about the money — the one you have almost forgotten — came when you were very hard up. And what you promised to do for old So-and-So and have never done — well, you never would have promised if you had known how frightfully busy you were going to be. And as for your behaviour to your wife (or husband) or sister (or brother) if I knew how irritating they could be, I would not wonder at it — and who the dickens am I, anyway? I am just the same. That is to say, I do not succeed in keeping the Law of Nature very well, and the moment anyone tells me I am not keeping it, there starts up in my mind a string of excuses as long as your arm. The question at the moment is not whether they are good excuses. The point is that they are one more proof of how deeply, whether we like it or not, we believe in the Law of Nature. If we do not believe in decent behaviour, why should we be so anxious to make excuses for not having behaved decently? The truth is, we believe in decency so much — we feel the Rule or Law pressing on us so — that we cannot bear to face the fact that we are breaking it, and consequently we try to shift the responsibility. For you notice that it is only for our bad behaviour that we find all these explanations. It is only our bad temper that we put down to being tired or worried or hungry; we put our good temper down to ourselves.[221]

Here is another thought, by President Benson, similar to Elder McConkie's previous statement:

How do you learn the commandments? You learn the commandments through the words of the Lord in the scriptures, through the revelations received by His authorized servants, through the Light of Christ, like a conscience that comes to every man, and through personal revelation.[222]

It seems that C.S. Lewis is really saying essentially the same thing — only in different words. Morality isn't an invention of man, and it's not something totally relative that vacillates from one culture to another, or from one time period to another. Even atheists and relativists would agree that basic human nature has not really changed throughout history. Ezra Taft Benson related the moral law to God, in connection with freedom in the following way:

I believe with all my heart the words of the American patriot Patrick Henry, who, on the eve of the American Revolution, said, "There is a just God who presides over the destinies of nations and who will raise up friends to fight our battles for us." Further, it is part of my faith that no people can maintain freedom unless their political institutions are founded on faith in God and belief in the existence of moral law. God has endowed men with certain inalienable rights, and no government may morally limit or destroy these.[223]

Here are some wise additional insights from Ezra Taft Benson:

Times are different, but fundamentals remain unchanged. Honesty is still honesty. Virtue is still virtue. Truth is still truth. Honest effort is still rewarded. Gravity still pulls all things to earth. Disregard for law still brings punishment. Two and two still make four. The Ten Commandments are still in force, as are all the other laws of life, nature, and the universe. Cecil B. DeMille once said that men and nations cannot break the Ten Commandments; they can only break themselves upon them.[224]

C.S. Lewis also wrote:

These, then, are the two points I wanted to make. First, that human beings, all over the earth, have this curious idea that they ought to behave in a certain way, and cannot really get rid of it. Secondly, that they do not in fact behave in that way. They know the Law of Nature; they break it. These two facts are the foundation of all clear thinking about ourselves and the universe we live in.[225]

This view is refreshing; he simply tells it like it is. C.S. Lewis also implies fundamental principles of agency and our inherent knowledge of right and wrong. Note the following from Bruce R. McConkie:

Truth is absolute and eternal; it endureth forever. (D&C 1:39; 88:66; Ps. 100:5; 117:2) It never varies; what is true in one age is true in every age. The theories of men (scientific or otherwise) vary from discovery to discovery and are in a continuing state of flux, unless they chance on a particular point to reach ultimate truth. Then there is no more change, and the truth discovered is in complete harmony with every other truth in every other field. Truth never conflicts with truth.[226]

Now compare that with more from C.S. Lewis:

Other people wrote to me saying, "Isn't what you call the Moral Law just a social convention, something that is put into us by education?" I think there is a misunderstanding here. The people who ask that question are usually taking it for granted that if we have learned a thing from parents and teachers, then that thing must be merely a human invention. But, of course, that is not so.[227]

Here is another jewel for comparison form Elder McConkie:

> Truth is not relative; it is absolute. What is true in one eternity is true in the next. The knowledge men have of the truth may be great at one time and slight in another, or the reverse, but the quantity of ultimate truth is neither added to nor diminished from by revelations received or discoveries made.[228]

More from C.S. Lewis:

> When you think about these differences between the morality of one people and another, do you think that the morality of one people is ever better or worse than that of another? Have any of the changes been improvements? If not, then of course there could never be any moral progress. Progress means not just changing, but changing for the better. If no set of moral ideas were truer or better than any other, there would be no sense in preferring civilized morality to savage morality, or Christian morality to Nazi morality. In fact, of course, we all do believe that some moralities are better than others. We do believe that some of the people who tried to change the moral ideas of their own age were what we would call Reformers or Pioneers — people who understood morality better than their neighbours did. Very well then. The moment you say that one set of moral ideas can be better than another, you are, in fact, measuring them both by a standard, saying that one of them conforms to that standard more nearly than the other. But the standard that measures two things is something different from either. You are, in fact, comparing them both with some Real Morality, admitting that there is such a thing as a real Right, independent of what people think, and that some people's ideas get nearer to that real Right, than others. Or put it this way. If your moral ideas can be truer, and those of the Nazis less true, there must be something — some Real Morality — for them to be true about. The reason why your idea of New York can be truer or less true than mine is that New York is a real place, existing quite apart from what either of us thinks. If when each of us said "New York" each meant merely "The town I am imagining in my own head," how could one of us have truer ideas than the other? There would be no question of truth or falsehood at all. In the same way, if the Rule of Decent Behaviour meant simply "whatever each nation happens to approve," there would be no sense in saying that any one nation had ever been more correct in its approval than any other; no sense in saying that the world could ever grow morally better or morally worse.[229]

And to complement the above, take the following from *The Abolition of Man* by C.S. Lewis:

> The human mind has no more power of inventing a new value than of imagining a new primary colour, or, indeed, of creating a new sun and a new sky for it to move in...[230]

Here is another from the same man:

> God may be more than moral goodness: He is not less. The road to the promised land runs past Sinai. The moral law may exist to be transcended: but there is no transcending it for those who have not first admitted its claims upon them, and then tried with all their strength to meet that claim, and fairly and squarely faced the fact of their failure. *(The Problem of Pain,* pg.65)

Also consider this, another ibid:

> ...every moral failure is going to cause trouble, probably to others and certainly to yourself. By talking about rules and obedience instead of "ideals" and "idealism" we help to remind ourselves of these facts.[231]

Now let me divert your attention for a moment into the doctrine of personal accountability and suffering for sins. Apparently, in C.S. Lewis' generation, as it is in ours, personal accountability began slipping into limbo somewhere. It seems to be the enlightened view now that to punish is somehow inhumane and barbaric. What does C.S. Lewis have to say on the subject?

> A perception of this truth lies at the back of the universal human feeling that bad men ought to suffer. It is no use turning up our noses at this feeling, as if it were wholly base. On its mildest level it appeals to everyone's sense of justice...On a sterner level the same idea appears as "retributive punishment," or "giving a man what he deserves." Some enlightened people would like to banish all conception of retribution or desert from their theory of punishment and place its value wholly in the deterrence of others of the reform of the criminal himself. They do not see that by so doing they render all punishment unjust. What can be more immoral than to inflict suffering on me for the sake of deterring others if I do not deserve it? And if I do deserve it, you are admitting the claims of "retribution." And what can be more outrageous than to catch me and submit me to a disagreeable process of moral improvement without my consent, unless (once more) I deserve it?[232]

Where is justice if people are not held responsible for what they do? The scriptures tell us that mercy "overpowereth justice" and therefore is perhaps a more exalted principle. However, the scriptures also, in unequivocal terms, say that mercy cannot rob justice. Recall Alma's words from *The Book of Mormon*:

> 13 Therefore, according to justice, the plan of redemption could not be brought about, only on conditions of repentance of men in this probationary state, yea, this preparatory state; for except it were for these conditions, mercy could not take effect except it should destroy the work of justice. Now the work of justice could not be destroyed; if so, God would cease to be God.
>
> And thus we see that all mankind were fallen, and they were in the grasp of justice; yea, the justice of God, which consigned them forever to be cut off from his presence.
>
> And now, the plan of mercy could not be brought about except an atonement should be made; therefore God himself atoneth for the sins of the world, to bring about the plan of mercy, to appease the demands of justice, that God might be a perfect, just God, and a merciful God also.
>
> Now, repentance could not come unto men except there were a punishment, which also was eternal as the life of the soul should be, affixed opposite to the plan of happiness, which was as eternal also as the life of the soul.
>
> Now, how could a man repent except he should sin? How could he sin if there was no law? How could there be a law save there was a punishment?
>
> Now, there was a punishment affixed, and a just law given, which brought remorse of conscience unto man.
>
> Now, if there was no law given — if a man murdered he should die — would he be afraid he would die if he should murder?
>
> And also, if there was no law given against sin men would not be afraid to sin.
>
> And if there was no law given, if men sinned what could justice do, or mercy either, for they would have no claim upon the creature?
>
> But there is a law given, and a punishment affixed, and a repentance granted; which repentance mercy claimeth; otherwise, justice claimeth the creature and executeth the law, and the law inflicteth the punishment; if not so, the works of justice would be destroyed, and God would cease to be God.

But God ceaseth not to be God, and mercy claimeth the penitent, and mercy cometh because of the atonement; and the atonement bringeth to pass the resurrection of the dead; and the resurrection of the dead bringeth back men into the presence of God; and thus they are restored into his presence, to be judged according to their works, according to the law and justice.

For behold, justice exerciseth all his demands, and also mercy claimeth all which is her own; and thus, none but the truly penitent are saved.

What, do ye suppose that mercy can rob justice? I say unto you, Nay; not one whit. If so, God would cease to be God.[233]

In the History of the Church we have additional insights as to how the Lord regards our obedience to His natural law, or more accurately, spiritual law.

This, then, was the nature of their offenses; they sinned against the Lord in the particulars named; they sinned against each other in the manner described; they did not trespass against their non-Mormon neighbors, nor break the laws of the land; but they failed to live in accordance with the high moral and spiritual law of the Gospel; they failed to meet the conditions on which God was pledged to their maintenance upon the land of Zion, and hence were left in the hands of their enemies.[234]

Every people of every culture everywhere and in every time *is* responsible to God to live up to the light and knowledge that they have. If they have been given little, their standard is lower and they will not be held as responsible. However, where much is given, much is required. Take the Nephites of old, for example. After the Lord visited, they lived in a glorious Zion society for 200 years. When the people finally revolted against that society, their case became awful, the Spirit left them, and then came speedy destruction. We know from modern revelation that once someone has had the heavens opened to them, and received great light and knowledge, if they then rebel against God, it would have been better for them never to have been born. Judas' sin was far greater than Pilate's.

The reason Lucifer's fate was so awful and so final was that he was in the presence of God himself, and rebelled. He was in the presence of perfect and absolute moral goodness, and rebelled against *that*. The *Doctrine and Covenants* describes the event like this:

And this we saw also, and bear record, that an angel of God who was in authority in the presence of God, who rebelled against the Only Begotten Son whom the Father loved and who was in the bosom of the Father, was thrust down from the presence of God and the Son,

And was called Perdition, for the heavens wept over him — he was Lucifer, a son of the morning.

And we beheld, and lo, he is fallen! is fallen, even a son of the morning!

And while we were yet in the Spirit, the Lord commanded us that we should write the vision; for we beheld Satan, that old serpent, even the devil, who rebelled against God, and sought to take the kingdom of our God and his Christ —

Yea, verily, the only ones who shall not be redeemed in the due time of the Lord, after the sufferings of his wrath.[235]

President Ezra Taft Benson asserted that no people could maintain their freedom if they rejected the moral law or the laws of God. He said, "I believe that no people can maintain freedom unless their political institutions are founded upon faith in God and belief in the existence of moral law."[236] As we believe, and as C.S. Lewis believed, when we try to reject or rationalize ourselves out of the moral law, we are in peril. And, when we knowingly rebel against God, we are in great peril.

...the spirits of those who are
righteous are received into a
state of happiness...

— Alma 40:12

CHAPTER 18

Happiness in the Gospel

The search for happiness has always been the foremost pursuit
of mankind, yet most of the searching everywhere, and in every age
of the world has been in vain. People have sought happiness by
chasing money and treasure, only to be sadly disillusioned in the
end. Some have tried to catch happiness by chasing every pleasure
that the world has to offer and by indulging, without restraint, in all
sorts of activities. These have also missed joy entirely, and found in
the end only corruption and ruin. David O. McKay said, "Actions in
harmony with divine law and the laws of nature will bring happiness, and those in opposition to divine truth, misery."[237]

C.S. Lewis had a remarkable understanding of how and where to
find happiness. He knew that true happiness could only be found by
living the gospel of Jesus Christ. His insights are nothing less than
inspired. He once wrote, "...a consistent practice of virtue by the
human race even for ten years would fill the earth from pole to pole
with peace, plenty, health, merriment, and heartease, and...nothing
else will." *(The Problem of Pain,* pg.63-64) In a nutshell, that is why
God calls prophets, organizes His church, calls us to repentance, and
issues commandments. It is all for the lasting happiness to be found
on earth and especially the joys of eternal life hereafter. C.S. Lewis
understood, as Alma did, that "wickedness never was happiness."
Compare his conclusions with those of Ezra Taft Benson:

> Only the gospel will save the world from the calamity of its
> own self-destruction. Only the gospel will unite men of all races
> and nationalities in peace. Only the gospel will bring joy, happi-
> ness, and salvation to the human family.[238]

President Benson also spoke of the spiritual illumination that
comes to people who live this gospel:

There is an inner light manifested in the countenances of those who have sought and found truth, who have set standards and principles in their lives and have been enlightened by the light of the gospel — hence, the brightness and spiritual illumination of those who have learned of and accepted the gospel of Jesus Christ.[239]

C.S. Lewis understood not only that happiness comes through following the Lord, but also the widespread, universal nature of the gospel. He wrote:

[Christianity] is an "eternal gospel" revealed to men wherever men have sought, or endured, the truth: it is the very nerve of redemption, which anatomising wisdom at all times and in all places lays bare the unescapable knowledge which the Light that lighteneth every man presses down upon the minds of all who seriously question what the universe is "about."[240]

He calls it an "eternal gospel" and then calls it the nerve of redemption. He understood that ultimately it is only people who submit to the gospel that can be redeemed. C.S. Lewis speaks of those "who seriously question what the universe is about." In other words, seekers of truth. Sometimes truth is very hard, even tedious. But those who embrace it find "wisdom and great treasures of knowledge," while those who seek the things of the world find the world, only to realize it never quite satisfied them. President Benson once gave a Christmas message in which he spoke of the advantages of living the gospel, and the disadvantages of not living it:

The Lord wants us to be happy. He will do His part if we will do our part. The Christlike life is the life that brings true happiness. There is no true happiness without God. Sin brings sorrow, disappointment, and heartaches. Only the good life brings a happy new year. It pays to live the gospel of Jesus Christ. It pays to accept the teachings of the Master, to apply them in our lives, to be true to the standards of the Church, to be true to our covenants — to live the gospel. And if we do this we will be bigger and can be bigger than anything that can possibly happen to us. I am sure that is the desire of all of us because those who have this faith, and have a testimony of the divinity of this work, can endure anything and keep their spirits sweet.[241]

He said that "sin brings sorrow, disappointment, and heartaches." That is the price of sin. Spencer W. Kimball spoke of the price of happiness when he said:

"What is the price of happiness?" One might be surprised at the simplicity of the answer. The treasure house of happiness is unlocked to those who live the gospel of Jesus Christ in its purity and simplicity. Like a mariner without stars, like a traveler without a compass, is the person who moves along through life without a plan. The assurance of supreme happiness, the certainty of a successful life here and of exaltation and eternal life hereafter, come to those who plan to live their lives in complete harmony with the gospel of Jesus Christ — and then consistently follow the course they have set. [242]

A traveler without a compass could be compared to someone who does not live the gospel, but looks to other means for happiness. C.S. Lewis exhibited wise understanding on this matter when he wrote:

> God made us: invented us as a man invents an engine. A car is made to run on gasoline, and it would not run properly on anything else. Now God designed the human machine to run on Himself. He Himself is the fuel our spirits were designed to burn, or the food our spirits were designed to feed on. There is no other. That is why it is just no good asking God to make us happy in our own way without bothering about religion. God cannot give us a happiness and peace apart from Himself, because it is not there. There is no such thing. [243]

How could God "make us happy in our own way?" Our own way is usually a detour off the path that leads to joy. And, sometimes we want so badly to be made happy in our own way and according to our own terms. In extreme cases, perhaps we, like the Nephites in Mormon's time, want God to give us happiness in sin. Sin and darkness are contrary to the very nature of happiness which was built into our souls when we were created. We cannot undo our own inherent nature, but we can cut ourselves off from the fountain of living water, the wellspring of all happiness.

Sometimes societies and governments try to make the people happy through programs, plans, policies, etc. Both C.S. Lewis and President Benson address this issue in similar and inspiring ways. First from President Benson:

> The Lord works from the inside out. The world works from the outside in. The world would take people out of the slums. Christ takes the slums out of people, and then they take themselves out of the slums. The world would mold men by changing their environment. Christ changes men, who then change their environment. The world would shape human behavior, but Christ can change human nature. [244]

Compare this with C.S. Lewis:

> ...all that thinking will be mere moonshine unless we realize that nothing but the courage and unselfishness of individuals is ever going to make any system work properly. It is easy enough to remove the particular kinds of graft or bullying that go on under the present system: but as long as men are twisters or bullies they will find some new way of carrying on the old game under the new system. You cannot make men good by law: and without good men you cannot have a good society. That is why we must go on to think of the second thing: or morality inside the individual.[245]

If people are determined to be wicked, or beat the system, or engage in any kind of mischief, government programs aimed at stopping this will be futile in the end. The gospel is the answer: faith, hope, charity, longsuffering, patience, love, humility, and all the rest are essential in the great final product of a happy soul. C.S. Lewis further comments on the futility of external conditions in bringing happiness:

> ...if people have not got at least the beginnings of those qualities inside them, then no possible external condition could make a "Heaven" for them — that is, could make them happy with the deep, strong, unshakable kind of happiness God intends for us.[246]

Elder Mark E. Peterson offers this:

> Are we to remain so blind and so stubborn that we will refuse to acknowledge our mistakes and humbly turn to the only source of true joy and happiness?[247]

C.S. Lewis also said, "I do not doubt that whatever misery He permits will be for our ultimate good unless by rebellious[ness] will we convert it to evil."[248]

Here we rediscover another profound principle. The essentials of happiness must begin within us. These essentials can never be found "out there" somewhere, if we do not have the elements of happiness already in our soul. In the next excerpt from *Mere Christianity*, C.S. Lewis deals with what there is for us outside of the gospel:

> What Satan put into the heads of our remote ancestors was the idea that they could 'be like gods' — could set up on their own as if they had created themselves — be their own masters — invent some sort of happiness for themselves outside God, apart from God. And out of that hopeless attempt has come nearly all that we

call human history — money, poverty, ambition, war, prostitution, classes, empires, slavery — the long terrible story of man trying to find something other than God which will make him happy.[249]

That is what the gospel is all about, and that is why God tries to refine us like gold — into something that can be capable of joy. The dross within us, such things as pride, avarice, and selfishness, are holding us back from that happiness which could be ours if we will only let ourselves be refined — painful though that may be. Following is another perspective on happiness from C.S. Lewis:

> When we want to be something other than the thing God wants us to be, we must be wanting what, in fact, will not make us happy. Those Divine demands which sound to our natural ears most like those of a despot and least like those of a lover, in fact marshall us where we should want to go if we know what we wanted. He demands our worship, our obedience, our prostration. The idea of reaching 'a good life' without Christ is based on a double error. Firstly, we cannot do it; and secondly, in setting up 'a good life' as our final goal, we have missed the very point of our existence. Morality is a mountain which we cannot climb by our own efforts; and if we could we should only perish in the ice and the unbreathable air of the summit, lacking those wings with which the rest of the journey has to be accomplished. For it is from there that the real ascent begins. The ropes and axes are 'done away' and the rest is a matter of flying.[250]

Here is an interesting comment about the people themselves who C.S. Lewis conceptualizes as righteous or holy:

> How little people know who think that holiness is dull. When one meets the real thing...it is irresistible. If even ten per cent of the world's population had it, would not the whole world be converted and happy before a year's end?[251]

Here is another perspective by the same:

> If you want joy, power, peace, eternal life, you must get close to, or even into, the thing that has them. They are not a sort of prize which God could, if He chose, just hand out to anyone. They are a great fountain of energy and beauty spurting up at the very centre of reality. If you are close to it, the spray will wet you: If you are not, you will remain dry. Once a man is united to God, how could he not live forever? Once a man is separated from God, what can he do but wither and die?[252]

Eternal Life, in some ways, is probably as much of a state of mind as Hell is. To enjoy eternal life, we've got to be the kind of people that have eternal life already inside of us, through living the gospel. C.S. Lewis also ends the above excerpt with a profound commentary on spiritual death. Through the gospel restored by Joseph Smith we know that this is precisely the definition of spiritual death: separation from God. Bruce R. McConkie offers the following:

> By definition, "the death of the spirit is for the spirit to die as to things pertaining to righteousness and consequently reap the damnation of hell. (2 Ne. 9:10-12) Utter spiritual ruin is thus imposed upon the soul; it is a lost soul, one that has not filled the measure of its creation. Lucifer's self-imposed mission is to destroy the souls of men (D&C 10:27), and his own ultimate destruction will come when he and his angels are cast into the lake of fire. (D&C 19:3; 2 Ne. 9:16)[253]

The Book of Mormon says the following:

> Behold, I say unto you that ye would be more miserable to dwell with a holy and just God, under a consciousness of your filthiness before him, than ye would to dwell with the damned souls in hell. (Mormon 9:4)

As part of becoming what we need to in order to have happiness and to be able to enjoy God's gifts, C.S. Lewis says that two necessary ingredients are obedience and cheerfulness. He writes:

> [A Christian society] is always insisting on obedience — obedience (and outward marks of respect) from all of us to properly appointed magistrates, from children to parents, and (I am afraid this is going to be very unpopular) from wives to husbands. Thirdly, it is to be a cheerful society: full of singing and rejoicing, and regarding worry or anxiety as wrong.[254]

Let us look at some parallel truths from Brigham Young and Bruce R. McConkie:

> I exhort you, masters, fathers, and husbands, to be affectionate and kind to those you preside over. And let them be obedient, let the wife be subject to her husband, and the children to their parents. Mothers, let your minds be sanctified before the Lord, for this is the commencement, the true foundation of a proper education in your children, the beginning point to form a disposition in

your offspring, that will bring honor, glory, comfort, and satisfaction to you all your lifetime.[255]

Also:

Music is part of the language of the Gods. It has been given to man so he can sing praises to the Lord. It is a means of expressing, with poetic words and in melodious tunes, the deep feelings of rejoicing and thanksgiving found in the hearts of those who have testimonies of the divine Sonship and who know of the wonders and glories wrought for them by the Father, Son, and Holy Spirit. Music is both in the voice and in the heart. Every true saint finds his heart full of songs of praise to his Maker. Those whose voices can sing forth the praises found in their hearts are twice blest. "Be filled with the Spirit," Paul counseled, "Speaking to yourselves in psalms and hymns and spiritual songs singing and making melody in your heart to the Lord." (Eph. 5:18-19) Also: "Let the word of Christ dwell in you richly in all wisdom; teaching and admonishing one another in psalms and hymns and spiritual songs, singing with grace in your hearts to the Lord." (Col. 3:16)[256]

And from the *Doctrine and Covenants*:

If thou art merry, praise the Lord with singing, with music, with dancing, and with a prayer of praise and thanksgiving. (D&C 136:28)

Now let us divert our attention for a moment into something that will probably surprise you. The United Order is something totally unique to the gospel of Jesus Christ restored by Joseph Smith, although something like it was practiced after Christ's coming, both in ancient America, and in ancient Israel. The United Order, in brief, is a system established by the Lord to exalt the poor and bring down the rich, that all might be equal. This was done by everyone giving everything they owned to a bishop or other supervisor, and then having that property and wealth redistributed to everyone according to their needs. Now being raised in America, the land of opportunity, and being taught the benefits of capitalism, I always secretly thought that the United Order sounded a lot like communism or socialism. The truth is, Satan has a close counterfeit to just about everything given by God. And communism is perhaps Satan's counterfeit to the United Order. In the following excerpt, C.S. Lewis is speculating about what it would be like to actually see a society that fully lived the gospel of Jesus Christ.

If there were such a society in existence and you or I visited it, I think we should come away with a curious impression. We should feel that its economic life was very socialistic and, in that sense, "advanced," but that its family life and its code of manners were rather old-fashioned — perhaps even ceremonious and aristocratic. Each of us would like some bits of it, but I am afraid very few of us would like the whole thing.[257]

Of the socialistic aspect, Bruce R. McConkie wrote:

To our Church members we say: Communism is not the United Order, and bears only the most superficial resemblance thereto; communism is based upon intolerance and force, the United Order upon love and freedom of conscience and action; communism involves forceful despoliation and confiscation, the United Order voluntary consecration and sacrifice.[258]

Interesting, isn't it?

But the natural man receiveth not the things of the Spirit of God: for they are foolishness unto him: neither can he know [them], because they are spiritually discerned.

— 1 Corinthians 2:14

CHAPTER 19

The Natural Man

Latter-day Saints understand God's purpose for them here in this mortal life and therefore differ somewhat with much of the world in their thinking about what we are here to do. You could say our primary mission, individually speaking, is to "put off the natural man" and become a new person — a child of Christ. Many Christians throughout the world have a sort of belief that God is like a schoolmaster; He is keeping score in heaven of our good deeds and bad, punishing us for our bad, smiling on our good, and at the end — seeing which way the balance tips. If it tips a little on the good side, we get Heaven, and if a little on the bad side, Hell. This philosophy is more fairy tale than truth, and C.S. Lewis understood it well. We are here to be refined like gold and molded like clay. It's not so much a matter of chalking up good points, as becoming a good creature. This change is a painful metamorphosis. Here's what C.S. Lewis has to say about it:

> We are not merely imperfect creatures who must be improved: we are, as Newman said, rebels who must lay down our arms. The first answer, then, to the question why our cure should be painful, is that to render back the will which we have so long claimed for our own, is in itself, wherever and however it is done, a grievous pain...But to surrender a self-will inflamed and swollen with years of usurpation is a kind of death. We all remember this self-will as it was in childhood, the bitter, prolonged rage at every thwarting, the burst of passionate tears, the black, Satanic wish to kill or die rather than to give in.[259]

Baptism itself is symbolic of burying the old person, and coming forth as a new person with the attributes of God. To do this, we must yield to the invitations and commands of the Holy Ghost. An angel delivered the following message to King Benjamin:

> For the natural man is an enemy to God, and has been from the fall of Adam, and will be, forever and ever, unless he yields to the enticings of the Holy Spirit, and putteth off the natural man and becometh a saint through the atonement of Christ the Lord, and becometh as a child, submissive, meek, humble, patient, full of love, willing to submit to all things which the Lord seeth fit to inflict upon him, even as a child doth submit to his father. (Mosiah 3:19)

Elder Neal A. Maxwell expounds on the doctrine of the natural man in these words:

> Though merciful, God has set strict and clear conditions for our returning to His presence. One of these conditions is that we are to become enlightened as little children — in the best spiritual sense of the word. There is a difference between childishness and meek, perceptive childlikeness. In childishness there is a profound possessiveness: "That's my toy!" There is open striving to be favored and ascendant: "That's my place!" Unchecked, these and other tendencies — unabated in the child — soon harden into the natural man, who is "an enemy to God" (Mosiah 3:19). The natural man is actually at cross purposes with God's plans. The natural man really has different ends, seeks different outcomes, marches to different drummers. If unrepentant, such become "carnal and devilish, and the devil has power over them" (Mosiah 16:3).[260]

He wrote the following in regards to the natural man and taking upon us the yoke of Christ:

> If we enlist and take the Savior's yoke upon us we "shall find rest unto [our] souls." (Matthew 11:29) If we are only part-time soldiers, though, partially yoked, we experience quite the opposite: frustration, irritation, and the absence of His full grace and spiritual rest. In that case weaknesses persist and satisfactions are intermittent. The less involved members resemble cartoonist Bill Mauldin's proud garritroopers of World War II — those who were too far forward to wear ties, but too far back to get shot, yet regarded themselves as real soldiers in the midst of the fray! Actually the partially yoked experience little spiritual satisfaction, because they are burdened by carrying the awful weight of the natural man — without any of the joys that come from

progressing toward becoming "the man of Christ." They have scarcely "[begun] to be enlightened" (Alma 32:34). The meek and fully yoked, on the other hand, find God's reassuring grace and see their weakness yielding to strength (see Ether 12:27).[261]

Following is an additional insight from Elder Maxwell:

A prominent feature of the natural man is selfishness — the inordinate and excessive concern with self. Prophets frequently warn about the dangers of this sin. The distance between constant self-pleasing and self-worship is shorter than we think. Stubborn selfishness is actually rebellion against God, because, warned Samuel, "stubbornness is as...idolatry" (1 Samuel 15:23).[262]

And another:

Such is the scope of putting off the burdensome natural man (see Mosiah 3:19), who is naturally selfish. So much of our fatigue in fact comes from carrying that needless load. This heaviness of the natural man prevents us from doing our Christian calisthenics; so we end up too swollen with selfishness to pass through the narrow needle's eye.[263]

One problem with putting off the natural man, other than being difficult in the first place, is that it usually doesn't work under conditions of ease and prosperity. Afflictions and trials, though unpleasant, are generally effective tools in the hand of God to produce the kind of mettle He wants in His saints. C.S. Lewis understood this as well. He wrote:

The human spirit will not even begin to try to surrender self-will as long as all seems to be well with it. Now error and sin both have this property, that the deeper they are the less their victim suspects their existence; they are masked evil. Pain is unmasked, unmistakable evil; every man knows that something is wrong when he is being hurt.[264]

There is hard evidence for this idea in the words of the Lord to the ancient American prophet Nephi:

And the Lord God said unto me: They shall be a scourge unto thy seed, to stir them up in remembrance of me; and inasmuch as they will not remember me, and hearken unto my words, they shall scourge them even unto destruction. (2 Nephi 5:25)

Apparently, the Lord is very serious about changing our natures. He says we will either change or, in the end, be destroyed. This is the serious business of our mortal probation, and it is God's work and His glory to change us into the kinds of beings that can experience joy everlastingly. C.S. Lewis describes his own struggle with the natural man in the following unique way:

> My own experience is something like this. I am progressing along the path of life in my ordinary contentedly fallen and godless condition, absorbed in a merry meeting with my friends for the morrow or a bit of work that tickles my vanity today, a holiday or a new book, when suddenly a stab of abdominal pain that threatens serious disease or a headline in the newspapers that threatens us all with destruction, sends this whole pack of cards tumbling down. At first I am overwhelmed, and all my little happiness looked like broken toys. Then slowly and reluctantly, bit by bit, I try to bring myself into the frame of mind that I should be in at all times. I remind myself that all these toys were never intended to possess my heart, that my true good is in another world and my only real treasure is Christ. And perhaps, by God's grace, I succeed, and for a day or two become a creature consciously dependent on God and drawing its strength from the right sources. But the moment the threat is withdrawn, my whole nature leaps back to the toys: I am even anxious, God forgive me, to banish from my mind the only thing that supported me under the threat because it is now associated with the misery of those few days. Thus the terrible necessity of tribulation is only too clear. God has had me for but forty-eight hours and then only by dint of taking everything else away from me. Let Him but sheathe that sword for a moment and I behave like a puppy when the hated bath is over — I shake myself as dry as I can and race off to reacquire my comfortable dirtiness, if not in the nearest manure heap, at least in the nearest flower bed. And that is why tribulation cannot cease until God either sees us remade or sees that our remaking is now hopeless.[265]

Most of the time we don't particularly *want* to be remade — just to be left alone with our toys and pleasures, and to go on being regular people. C.S. Lewis also hits on one of the primary themes of *The Book of Mormon* in the preceding excerpt — that while God is chastening us, we tend to turn to Him, but as soon as he lets us alone with peace, prosperity, and the good life, we turn back to ourselves. How many times were the Nephites "left alone" only to get wealthy, followed by getting prideful and eventually wicked? This seemed to be one eternal round with the Nephites. It happened over and over. And as C.S. Lewis understood, just as God works with nations in this manner, he works with each one of us individually. In Alma 46:8 we read, "Thus we see how quick the children of men do forget the Lord their God, yea, how quick to do iniquity, and to be led away by the evil one."

C.S. Lewis had a striking understanding of how repentance must come into play for the natural man. He wrote:

> Now what was the sort of "hole" man had got himself into? He had tried to set up on his own, to behave as if he belonged to himself. In other words, fallen man is not simply an imperfect creature who needs improvement; he is a rebel who must lay down his arms. Laying down your arms, surrendering, saying you are sorry, realising that you have been on the wrong track and getting ready to start life over again from the ground floor — that is the only way out of a "hole." This process of surrender — this movement full speed astern — is what Christians call repentance. Now repentance is no fun at all. It is something much harder than merely eating humble pie. It means unlearning all the self-conceit and self-will that we have been training ourselves into for thousands of years. It means killing part of yourself, undergoing a kind of death. In fact, it needs a good man to repent. And here comes the catch. Only a bad person needs to repent: only a good person can repent perfectly. The worse you are the more you need it and the less you can do it. The only person who could do it perfectly would be a perfect person — and he would not need it.[266]

He did not subscribe to the belief of some schools of Christian thought which says all you need to do to obtain Heaven is say you believe in Jesus. You need no repentance, no righteous works, no effort even! How could this be real? C.S. Lewis understood the harsh realities along with the glorious possibilities. He understood what Joseph Smith taught: that the kind of people we become in this world will not magically change when we die, but will remain with us into the next world.

Now note some of the characteristics C.S. Lewis attributes to the natural man:

> The natural life in each of us is something self-centred, something that wants to be petted and admired, to take advantage of other lives, to exploit the whole universe. And especially it wants to be left to itself: to keep well away from anything better or stronger or higher than it, anything that might make it feel small. It is afraid of the light and air of the spiritual world, just as people

who have been brought up to be dirty are afraid of a bath. And in a sense it is quite right. It knows that if the spiritual life gets hold of it, all its self-centredness and self-will are going to be killed and it is ready to fight tooth and nail to avoid that.[267]

Perhaps we are afraid of some imagined and treasured part of ourselves that could be lost if we put off the natural man. But when we do lose it, we find it was nothing of much value in the first place, and we are given something far greater in return anyway. Compare the above insights on the natural man with those of Neal A. Maxwell following:

> WINSTON: It seems we must ever be watchful. The tilt and veer of the natural man is to one side or the other of the strait and narrow path.
>
> CHARLES: I need, for instance, to develop humility and meek-ness, but the tendency of us mortals is toward pride. We are to develop patience, but the natural man is impatient. We are to be pure, but the natural man tends toward corruption. We are to be spiritually submissive, but the natural man tends toward selfish-ness and aggressiveness. We are to endure well, but, left to our natural tendencies, we would give up.[268]

We now need to take a look at what C.S. Lewis offers us in the way of examining ourselves and finding the natural man. An enemy must first be identified if it is to be dealt with. This requires a fair amount of soul searching, and often times painful soul searching. The following is based on the idea that the *true* person within us is to be found when we are caught off guard, or slightly unprepared for any given difficult situation:

> …surely what a man does when he is taken off his guard is the best evidence for what sort of a man he is? Surely what pops out before the man has time to put on a disguise is the truth? If there are rats in a cellar you are most likely to see them if you go in very suddenly. But the suddenness does not create the rates: it only prevents them from hiding. In the same way the suddenness of the provocation does not make me an ill-tempered man: it only shows me what an ill-tempered man I am. The rats are always there in the cellar, but if you go in shouting and noisily they will have taken cover before you switch on the light. Apparently the rats of resent-ment and vindictiveness are always there in the cellar of my soul.[269]

Elder Maxwell commented on this very passage in one of his books:

Just as life itself is not abstract but very real, so family life plays back to us, constantly, our need to be better. There is wisdom in C.S. Lewis's reminder to us all that if we want to find out if there are rats in the cellar, then fling the cellar door open suddenly. We will never see the rats in the cellar if we go tromping down the hall, giving all kinds of warnings. Family life is not alone in giving us glimpses into the cellar of self, but, more than anywhere else, we are apt to have love and understanding and specific support as we try to get rid of the "rats," for such tasks can be family projects in which we are not left alone with the task.[270]

Now, consider what Joseph Fielding Smith said about trying to view ourselves in the natural state, and then about the joys that follow when we yield to the enticings of the Holy Spirit and become a saint:

While we are in mortality we are clogged, and we see as through a glass darkly, we see only in part, and it is difficult for us to comprehend the smallest things with which we are associated. But when we put on immortality, our condition will be very different, for we ascend into an enlarged sphere; although we shall not become perfect immediately after our departure from the body, for the spirit without the body is not perfect, and the body without the spirit is dead. The disembodied spirit during the interval of the death of the body and its resurrection from the grave is not perfect, hence it is not prepared to enter into the exaltation of the celestial kingdom; but it has the privilege of soaring in the midst of immortal beings, and of enjoying, to a certain extent, the presence of God, not the fulness of his glory, not the fulness of the reward which we are seeking and which we are destined to receive, if found faithful to the law of the celestial kingdom, but only in part.[271]

Confronting the natural man within us can be a terrible thing, but one with great rewards. But when we do search ourselves and come to the conclusion that we must end our rebellion, and hand ourselves over to God, we begin to taste the first hints of the tree of life. Ponder the following words by C.S. Lewis:

The terrible thing, the almost impossible thing, is to hand over your whole self — all your wishes and precautions — to Christ. But it is far easier than what we are all trying to do instead. For what we are trying to do is to remain what we call "ourselves," to keep personal happiness as our great aim in life, and yet at the same time be "good." We are all trying to let our mind and heart go their own way — centred on money or pleasure or ambition — and hoping, in spite of this, to behave honesty and chastely and humbly. And that is exactly what Christ warned us you could not do. As He said, a thistle cannot produce figs. If I am a field that contains nothing but grass-seed, I cannot produce wheat. Cutting the grass may keep it short: but I shall still produce grass and no wheat. If I want to produce wheat, the change must go deeper than the surface. I must be ploughed up and re-sown.

That is why the real problem of the Christian life comes where people do not usually look for it. It comes the very moment you wake up each morning. All your wishes and hopes for the day rush at you like wild animals. And the first job each morning consists simply in shoving them all back; in listening to that other voice, taking that other point of view, letting that other larger, stronger, quieter life come flowing in. And so on, all day. Standing back from all your natural fussings and frettings; coming in out of the wind.

We can only do it for moments at first. But from those moments the new sort of life will be spreading throughout our system: because now we are letting Him work at the right part of us. It is the difference between pain, which is merely laid on the surface, and a dye or stain which soaks right through. He never talked vague, idealistic gas. When he said, "Be perfect," He meant it. He meant that we must go in for the full treatment. It is hard; but the sort of compromise we are all hankering after is harder — in fact, it is impossible. It may be hard for an egg to turn into a bird: it would be a jolly sight harder for it to learn to fly while remaining an egg. We are like eggs at present. And you cannot go on indefinitely being just an ordinary, decent egg. We must be hatched or go bad.[272]

C.S. Lewis bravely squared himself with the doctrine of striving for perfection. Jesus commanded us to be perfect. We must have that as our goal, and nothing less. Christ wants us to aim at the stars. If we strive for perfection, it's an uphill battle all the way. But we're climbing to where the air is clear — we're climbing heavenward. In the preceding excerpt, C.S. Lewis spoke of handing over ourselves to God in exchange for a "self" that is much better. Compare his ideas with the principles taught by Elder Maxwell in the following:

Since, alas, a holding back regarding the hard doctrines does seem to be characteristic, why don't we at least resist equally the gravitational pull coming from the other direction? The adversary would claim us, too! Somehow he gets away with it, even though his way is monotony masquerading as individuality, and even though the selfishness he encourages is merely an apostate individualism.[273]

In the name of being different, some really become more and more alike until any real individuality is lost. The Good Shepherd taught, "He that findeth his life shall lose it: and he that loseth his life for my sake shall find it." (Matthew 10:39) Often, "doing your own thing" means simply to be marshalled into the enemy's camp and enticed to sin like everyone else. Again, Elder Maxwell offers us wisdom in this:

> Clearly, the worldly living epitomized by such a philosophy celebrates openly the selfish doing of one's own thing. Its conformity masquerades as individuality — a circumstance somewhat like goldfish in a bowl congratulating themselves on their self-sufficiency while unacknowledging of the one who puts in the food pellets and changes the water.[274]

C.S. Lewis also has wisdom for us with a similar thought:

> Until you have given up your self to Him you will not have a real self. Sameness is to be found most among the most "natural" men, not among those who surrender to Christ. How monotonously alike all the great tyrants and conquerors have been: how gloriously different are the saints.[275]

His words are eloquent and evident. In the following passage he says also that we must throw away ourselves "blindly" in order to find our true selves, implying a leap of faith.

> But there must be a real giving up of the self. You must throw it away "blindly" so to speak. Christ will indeed give you a real personality: but you must not go to Him for the sake of that. As long as your own personality is what you are bothering about you are not going to Him at all. The very first step is to try to forget about the self altogether. Your real, new self (which is Christ's and also yours, and yours just because it is His) will not come as long as you are looking for it. It will come when you are looking for Him. Does that sound strange? The same principle holds, you know, for more everyday matters. Even in social life, you will never make a good impression on other people until you stop thinking about what sort of impression you are making. Even in literature and art, no man who bothers about originality will ever be original: whereas if you simply try to tell the truth (without caring twopence how often it has been told before) you will, nine times out of ten, become original without ever having noticed it. The principle runs through all life from top to bottom. Give up your self, and you will find your real self. Lose your life and you will save it. Submit to death, death of your ambitions and

favourite wishes every day and death of your whole body in the end: submit with every fibre of your being, and you will find eternal life. Keep back nothing. Nothing that you have not given away will ever be really yours. Nothing in you that has not died will ever be raised form the dead. Look for yourself, and you will find in the long run only hatred, loneliness, despair, rage, ruin, and decay. But look for Christ and you will find Him, and with Him everything else thrown in.[276]

This seems to be a terribly accurate description of our war to overcome the natural man. The stakes are so high and the rewards are so great. Yet the war is comprised not of one great battle, but of a million tiny battles — every day and every hour of our lives. Of the entire process, C.S. Lewis wrote, "This process can be described either as an enlargement or as a temporary annihilation of the self. But that is an old paradox; 'he that loseth his life shall save it.'"[277]

C.S. Lewis believed that this quest for perfection was not merely a matter of taking the raw material we've already got and improving it, but that we must "become new creatures," completely discarding the old natural self and putting on the man of Christ. He said:

> For mere improvement is not redemption, though redemption always improves people even here and now and will, in the end, improve them to a degree we cannot yet imagine. God became man to turn creatures into sons: not simply to produce better men of the old kind but to produce a new kind of man. It is not like teaching a horse to jump better and better but like turning a horse into a winged creature. Of course, once it has got its wings, it will soar over fences which could never have been jumped and thus beat the natural horse at its own game.[278]

And others will he pacify, and lull
them away into carnal security, that
they will say: all is well in Zion;
yea, Zion prospereth, all is well —
and thus the devil cheateth their
souls, and leadeth them away
carefully down to hell.

— 2 Nephi 28:21

CHAPTER 20

Soft Religion

When our missionaries go all over the world preaching the restored gospel of Jesus Christ, they offer many things to people. They offer the truth about God and Jesus Christ. They offer what the real plan of salvation is all about. They offer a blueprint for peace in this life, and eternal life in the next. But one thing they do not offer is an easy life.

However, some Christian denominations offer an easy religion; one that requires very little effort or sacrifice. It seems that in some cases it is a matter of gaining popularity. Just like a politician tries to win voters by offering what the people want, so also do many ministers try to shape Christianity into something with wider appeal, whether or not this shaping conforms with the truth. C.S. Lewis looked on this kind of religion-shamming with contempt. He sought out the facts, and tried to align his life with the reality that is. Of the current religious sentiment in England he wrote:

> But one word of warning. There has been a great deal of soft soap talked about God for the last hundred years. That is not what I am offering. You can cut all that out.[279]

Now observe how he related this to the moral law and to God:

> The moral Law does not give us any grounds for thinking that God is "good" in the sense of being indulgent, or soft, or sympathetic. There is nothing indulgent about the Moral Law. It is as

hard as nails. It tells you to do the straight thing and it does not seem to care how painful, or dangerous, or difficult it is to do. If God is like the Moral Law, then He is not soft.[280]

Indeed, in reality, there must be opposition in all things. The Lord has promised that he will try our patience and our faith. Joseph Smith taught some of his closest confidants that God would wrench their very heartstrings, and if they could not bear it, they would not be fit for the kingdom of God.[281]

In reference to this concept of an easy religion, Hugh Nibley relates it to science in this way:

> The real enemy of true science is the glib and superficial lip service to science that goes under the name of liberalism. And the same holds true for religion. There is no substance to the easy and sentimental "religion of man" by which the human race was expected to lift itself to infinite heights by a gentle tugging on its own boot-straps.[282]

Religion isn't something only for Sunday: to be separated and compartmentalized from "real life." It is the truth and guiding force for our real life. We can't cut corners and soften edges when it comes to our faith. We must accept what already is and align our lives with that. In C.S. Lewis' book *The Screwtape Letters*, Screwtape gives more advice to his nephew Wormwood: "A moderated religion is as good for us as no religion at all — and more amusing." *(The Screwtape Letters*, pg.45) In *Mere Christianity*, C.S. Lewis wrote:

> If Christianity was something we were making up, of course we could make it easier. But it is not. We cannot compete, in simplicity, with people who are inventing religions. How could we? We are dealing with Fact. Of course anyone can be simple if he has no facts to bother about.[283]

This is happening all over the world, and most likely, this very day. When the leaders of a church begin to "vote" on doctrine, a religion is in the fabrication process. When religious panels or forums get together to decide upon the principles of their church, or a new direction to be taken by their congregation, without the aid of revelation, as C.S. Lewis says, they are "inventing religion." He also strongly believed that God desires our refining and perfection — not our immediate comfort. He wrote the following dealing with this idea:

What would really satisfy us would be a God who said of anything we happened to like doing, "What does it matter so long as they are contented?" We want, in fact, not so much a Father in Heaven as a grandfather in heaven — a senile benevolence who, as they say, "liked to see young people enjoying themselves," and whose plan for the universe was simply that it might be truly said at the end of each day, "a good time was had by all." Not many people, I admit, would formulate a theology in precisely those terms: but a conception not very different lurks at the back of many minds. I do not claim to be an exception: I should very much like to live in a universe which was governed on such lines. But since it is abundantly clear that I don't, and since I have reason to believe, nevertheless, that God is Love, I conclude that my conception of love needs correction. I might, indeed, have learned, even from the poets, that Love is something more stern and splendid than mere kindness. *(The Problem of Pain*, pg.40)

Twentieth century sociology and family science has produced for us the phrase "tough love," which means loving but not spoiling, pampering, or indulging. I think this tough love is an adequate description of what God has for us. Our Heavenly Father desires nothing so much as our eternal well being, but He does not always enforce our immediate comfort. In fact, His whole plan is designed around testing us and proving us, usually in the midst of afflictions hand tailored for us. In Zechariah 13:9 the Lord said: "And I will bring the third part through the fire, and will refine them as silver is refined, and will try them as gold is tried: they shall call on my name, and I will hear them: I will say, It [is] my people: and they shall say, The LORD [is] my God."

Many have criticized Christianity — and religion in general — on all manner of philosophical, scientific, and otherwise worldly grounds. Lehi saw in his dream people ridiculing those trying to follow the Lord. We see it happening today and it's been going on forever. C.S. Lewis, author turned defender of the faith, once wrote:

[Some] people put up a version of Christianity suitable for a child of six and make that the object of their attack. When you try to explain the Christian doctrine as it is really held by an instructed adult, they then complain that you are making their heads turn round and that it is all too complicated and that if there really were a God they are sure He would have made "religion" simple, because simplicity is so beautiful, etc. You must be on your guard against these people for they will change their ground every minute and only waste your time. Notice, to, their idea of god "making religion simple:" as if "religion" were something

God invented, and not His statement to us of certain quite unalterable facts about His own nature.[284]

Joseph Smith taught that God was once a man, going through the same processes of development that we are currently undergoing. Laws exist, principles are fixed, and God lives by these. If God arbitrarily made universal laws, then he could arbitrarily break them. But we know that God abides by law. *The Book of Mormon* teaches that if God were to break the law of justice, then he would cease to be God but, "He ceaseth not to be God."

That brings us to the issue of doctrine. And, like facts, doctrines are stubborn things. We cannot mold doctrines to our own liking, but we can mold ourselves to them. Of doctrines, Elder Neal A. Maxwell wrote:

> When one decides whether or not to deal with hard doctrines, the tendency is to put them off or to be put off by them. Not only are they in some respects puzzling, but they may even offend our mortal pride. Just as there are some good deeds we do gladly and quickly (while others are put off time and again), so it is with certain gospel truths: we accept some with joy and alacrity, but others we keep at arm's length. The hardness is usually not in their complexity, but in the deep demands these doctrines make of us. They are actually harder to accept than to understand, for there is a breathtaking simplicity about them. (*All These Things Shall Give Thee Experience*, pg.3-4)

Yes, the "hard doctrines" are seldom any fun at all, but we must embrace them if we want truth and eternal life. Loving one's enemies has never been one of the more popular or enjoyable doctrines, yet this the Master commanded, and this we must do. Elder Neal A. Maxwell continues:

> In any event, to ignore the hard doctrines deprives us of much-needed doctrinal rations for the rigorous journey...The central doctrines can quicken in us this desire for a full reunion. The hard sayings can help us in hard times, so that we do not lose the way. These sublime truths will enliven our consciences and stir our dimmed memories of promises made and vows taken — and at those very moments when we would otherwise be pulled from the path. These key truths, when kept before us, will lift our hopes and our eyes when we are downcast or in despair, and will lift our minds and thoughts from lower inclinations that are unworthy of who we are...So lifted, we can, afresh, see the distant but beckoning City of God on the hill. When weary legs falter and detours

and roadside allurements entice, the fundamental doctrines will summon from deep within us fresh determination. Extraordinary truths can move us to extraordinary accomplishments! And, strangely enough, even as we partake of the bread of adversity (with its unique calories), this will provide us with new and needed energy. The hard doctrines will also keep us from that flabbiness which has called a sad halt to many a journey — as well — doing individuals have grown "weary by the way."[285]

Those very principles we try to run away from because of their hardness may very well be crucial for our spiritual well being, either now or in the future. When we are downtrodden and discouraged, fiction is not nearly as is consoling as comforting truth. But, we must find and embrace the truth. C.S. Lewis wrote:

> If you look for truth, you may find comfort in the end: if you look for comfort you will not get either comfort or truth — only soft soap and wishful thinking to begin with and, in the end, despair. Most of us have got over the pre-war wishful thinking about international politics. It is time we did the same about religion.Very well then, atheism is too simple. And I will tell you another view that is also too simple. It is the view I call Christianity-and-water, the view which simply says there is a good God in Heaven and everything is all right — leaving out all the difficult and terrible doctrines about sin and hell and the devil, and the redemption. Both these are boys' philosophies.[286]

Korihor in *The Book of Mormon* thought along these lines. He said that nothing was really a sin, and we could do what we want. Also note the prophecy in 2 Nephi 28:8 —

> And there shall also be many which shall say: Eat, drink, and be merry; nevertheless, fear God — he will justify in committing a little sin; yea, lie a little, take the advantage of one because of his words, dig a pit for thy neighbor; there is no harm in this; and do all these things, for tomorrow we die; and if it so be that we are guilty, God will beat us with a few stripes, and at last we shall be saved in the kingdom of God.

C.S. Lewis never read *The Book of Mormon*, but he understood many of the universal teachings found within. He wrote:

> The god of whom no dogmas are believed is a mere shadow. He will not produce that fear of the Lord in which wisdom begins, and, therefore, will not produce that love in which it is consum-

mated....There is in this minimal religion nothing that can convince, convert, or (in the higher sense) console; nothing, therefore, which can restore vitality to our civilization. It is not costly enough. It can never be a controller or even a rival to our natural sloth and greed.[287]

The Prophet Joseph Smith taught that true religion must require sacrifice and be a vehicle through which we are pushed and stretched to our limits that we may reach our full potential. He taught that:

> ...a religion that does not require the sacrifice of all things never has power sufficient to produce the faith necessary unto life and salvation; for, from the first existence of man, the faith necessary unto the enjoyment of life and salvation never could be obtained without the sacrifice of all earthly things. It was through this sacrifice, and this only, that God has ordained that men should enjoy eternal life; and it is through the medium of the sacrifice of all earthly things that men do actually know that they are doing the things that are well pleasing in the sight of God. When a man has offered in sacrifice all that he has for the truth's sake, not even withholding his life, and believing before God that he has been called to make this sacrifice because he seeks to do his will, he does know, most assuredly, that God does and will accept his sacrifice and offering, and that he has not, nor will not seek his face in vain. Under these circumstances, then, he can obtain the faith necessary for him to lay hold on eternal life.[288]

Think what God required of Abraham, Abinadi, and Joseph Smith. This is a gospel in which the true God, if we choose to listen to Him, requires everything, and gives us back everything and more in the end. Abraham didn't sit on his sofa and talk about being saved. He went up on Mount Moriah to offer the greatest sacrifice God could have asked of him. Abinadi didn't look for the easiest religion he could find in his city; he followed the true and living God and was eventually asked to lay down his life for Him. Joseph Smith could have had a much easier life had he simply joined one of the churches in his area and been happy with that. But thank goodness he didn't. Where would the world be today without his work? C.S. Lewis wrote, "The presence which we voluntarily evade is often, and we know it, His presence in wrath." *(The Problem of Pain)* He wrote:

> And out of this evil comes a good. If I never fled from His presence, then I should suspect those moments when I seemed to delight in it of being wish-fulfillment dreams. That, by the way,

explains the feebleness of all those water versions of Christianity which leave out all the darker elements and try to establish a religion of pure consolation. No real belief in the watered versions can last. Bemused and besotted as we are, we still dimly know at heart that nothing which is at all times and in every way agreeable to us can have objective reality. It is of the very nature of the real that it should have sharp corners and rough edges, that it should be resistant, should be itself. Dream-furniture is the only kind on which you never stub your toes or bang your knee.[289]

C.S. Lewis spoke about a popular scientific concept — creative evolution. He wrote:

One reason why many people find Creative Evolution so attractive is that it gives one much of the emotional comfort of believing in God and none of the less pleasant consequences. When you are feeling fit and the sun is shining and you do not want to believe that the whole universe is a mere mechanical dance of atoms, it is nice to be able to think of this great mysterious Force rolling on through the centuries and carrying you on its crest. If on the other hand, you want to do something rather shabby, the Life-Force, being only a blind force, with no morals and no mind, will never interfere with you like that troublesome God we learned about when we were children. The Life-Force is a sort of tame God. You can switch it on when you want, but it will not bother you. All the thrills of religion and none of the cost. Is the Life-Force the greatest achievement of wishful thinking the world has yet seen?[290]

Compare his words with those of Hugh Nibley's below:

But what has happened? Those who have called themselves liberals in religion have accepted science with open arms precisely because they believe that excuses them from any toil at all. For them to have an open mind means to accept without question, and without any personal examination of evidence, whatever the prevailing opinions of the experts may prescribe. This is what Haldane calls prejudice. Evolution was hailed as the new gospel not because it raised new questions or spurred some men to new searches, but because for the man in the street and the lazy student, as well as for the people who wrote books for them, it meant the end of all searching and the end of all doubt. Here was the answer to everything, and no open-minded nonsense about it. I recently reviewed a two-volume work on ancient history in which the author had obviously not bothered to read more than a fraction of his sources. Why should he bother? By the evolutionary rule-of-thumb he could reconstruct the whole broad course of history with confidence and ease, oblivious to the disquieting fact that the documents, had he taken the trouble to read them, would have told him a very different story. Evolution was the conclusion on which he based his facts. The doctrine, however useful in other fields, has had a crippling, even a paralyzing effect on humanistic studies, where its ready-made answers to everything have spared students the pains and denied them the experience of finding out for themselves what the texts actually say.[291]

C.S. Lewis understood that truth is to be found in the doctrines of the gospel, and that these doctrines are not always easy. More often than not, the truth is hard — nevertheless, it will make us free. He held contempt for the ideas of "soft religion" in which people try to invent something that suits them and call it Christianity. He was interested in the truth about eternal and spiritual things — nothing less.

...and whom I love I also chasten...

— D&C 91:5

— CHAPTER 21 —

Man's Relationship with God

Man's relationship with God has been a puzzle that has evaded mankind for centuries. Only when the gospel is had in its fullness, or when people have some kind of a link with God (such as a prophet, or personal revelation), can they truly begin to discover what our relationship with God is. Philosophers have been trying to discover this forever through means of reason and logic. But this has proved mostly futile. Take for example the question that always seems to come up. "If God is good and loving, why does He allow so much suffering on the earth? Why does he allow little children to suffer and die?" The answer to these questions and others are all inseparably connected to our relationship with God. C.S. Lewis calls it the problem of pain. He wrote the following in his book *The Problem of Pain:*

> "If God were good, He would wish to make His creatures perfectly happy, and if God were almighty, He would be able to do what He wished. But the creatures are not happy. Therefore God lacks either goodness, or power, or both." This is the problem of pain in its simplest form.[292]

Of course, this type of shoddy reasoning has seemed strong enough to some — strong enough to lead them into atheism. Philosophers take the tidy premises above, stack them, wrap them, turn the crank, and out comes the only possible logical answer. The problem with it all is that the initial assumptions are without grounds. Where is it written that God wishes to make us all perfectly happy every moment? And, how can we assume that because God usually does not interfere with the agency of man, that this in some way limits His omnipotence? C.S. Lewis puts into words what many have felt about this dilemma:

> What would really satisfy us would be a God who said of anything we happened to like doing, "What does it matter so long as they are contented?" We want, in fact, not so much a Father in Heaven as a grandfather in heaven — a senile benevolence who,

as they say, "liked to see young people enjoying themselves," and whose plan for the universe was simply that it might be truly said at the end of each day, "a good time was had by all." Not many people, I admit, would formulate a theology in precisely those terms: but a conception not very different lurks at the back of many minds. I do not claim to be an exception: I should very much like to live in a universe which was governed on such lines. But since it is abundantly clear that I don't, and since I have reason to believe, nevertheless, that God is Love, I conclude that my conception of love needs correction. I might, indeed, have learned, even from the poets, that Love is something more stern and splendid than mere kindness.[293]

Our relationship with God is like a tutelage. Or, perhaps we could think of the Master as a loving drill sergeant. He lets us experience pain so that we can enjoy its opposite, and so that we will develop a sense of mercy for others who suffer. He lets us die that we might enjoy life eternal. He allows many things that we call "bad" for the same reasons that a drill sergeant constructs a difficult obstacle course — to train and toughen the troops. Lehi taught that there must be opposition in all things.[294] The Lord revealed to Joseph Smith the following truth about mankind's relationship to God:

> Behold, the great day of the Lord is at hand; and who can abide the day of his coming, and who can stand when he appeareth? For he is like a refiner's fire, and like fuller's soap; and he shall sit as a refiner and purifier of silver, and he shall purify the sons of Levi, and purge them as gold and silver, that they may offer unto the Lord an offering in righteousness...[295]

Our Heavenly Father is a refiner of us, his children. He wants to make us into the kind of people that can be exalted. In Doctrine & Covenants 18:10, God revealed, "Remember the worth of souls is great in the sight of God." And, in Moses 1:39, "For behold, this is my work and my glory — to bring to pass the immortality and eternal life of man." This is what the whole thing is about. This is why we are here. We can't become like God until we pass through the kinds of things He passed through, and develop the attributes of Him. C.S. Lewis keenly understood this truth. He wrote:

> Over a sketch made idly to amuse a child, an artist may not take much trouble: he may be content to let it go even though it is not exactly as he meant it to be. But over the great picture of his

life — the work which he loves, though in a different fashion, as intensely as man loves a woman or a mother a child — he will take endless trouble — and would, doubtless, thereby give endless trouble to the picture if it were sentient. One can imagine a sentient picture, after being rubbed and scraped and re-commenced for the tenth time, wishing that it were only a thumb-nail sketch whose making was over in a minute. In the same way, it is natural for us to wish that God had designed for us a less glorious and less arduous destiny; but then we are wishing not for more love but for less.[296]

The last line of the above paragraph exhibits his adept under-standing of God's work and His glory. The Lord could have made life every bit pleasant; He could have made a garden of Eden for all. But where is the love in that? Instead, He is making us into the kind of people that He is. In D&C 95:1, the Lord would have us under-stand that through chastening we can more ably have our sins forgiven. The passage reads:

> Verily, thus saith the Lord unto you whom I love, and whom I love I also chasten that their sins may be forgiven, for with the chastisement I prepare a way for their deliverance in all things out of temptation, and I have loved you —

The Lord chastens us because he loves us. C.S. Lewis wrote:

> We may wish, indeed, that we were of so little account to God that He left us alone to follow our natural impulses — that he would give over trying to train us into something so unlike our natural selves: but once again, we are asking not for more Love, but for less.[297]

Often it would seem easier for us if God left us alone, as C.S. Lewis said, "to follow our natural impulses." But this mortality is only a means to an end. The end itself is eternal life, and this earth is the proving ground on which God is trying to shape us into something everlastingly more valuable to ourselves and to Him. C.S. Lewis said that sometimes God would leave us alone. This is a natural inclination for all of us. Indeed, it was so even with our first parents, Adam and Eve:

> And they heard the voice of the Lord God, as they were walking in the garden, in the cool of the day; and Adam and his wife went to hide themselves from the presence of the Lord God amongst the trees of the garden.[298]

A moral is to be found for us in the story of Jonah, who tried to run away from the Lord, only to be tossed overboard from his ship and end up in the belly of a whale.

Many struggle with the idea of pain. Why does God allow it? Why is there so much pain in the world? C.S. Lewis offers a profound insight:

> But pain insists upon being attended to. God whispers to us in our pleasures, speaks in our conscience, but shouts in our pains: it is His megaphone to rouse a deaf world.[299]

How many of us would never turn to God if we were not awakened by this terrible tool? Alma the younger learned a hard lesson in pain and how it tends to turn us to God. He records:

> And it came to pass that I was three days and three nights in the most bitter pain and anguish of soul; and never, until I did cry out unto the Lord Jesus Christ for mercy, did I receive a remission of my sins. But behold, I did cry unto him and I did find peace to my soul. (Alma 38:8)

This one simple lesson is enough to slice through volumes of philosophical meanderings on the subject. True principles are not always pleasant principles, but they must be dealt with squarely if we are interested in reality. Alma called upon the Lord for mercy after three days of pain and anguish of soul. We are like him. Often we don't turn to God until all other methods prove futile, or until we can't bear whatever we're suffering anymore. C.S. Lewis wrote:

> Until the evil man finds evil unmistakably present in his existence, in the form of pain, he is enclosed in illusion. Once pain has roused him, he knows that he is in some way or other "up against" the real universe: he either rebels (with the possibility of a clearer issue and deeper repentance at some later stage) or else makes some attempt at an adjustment, which, if pursued, will lead him to religion....No doubt Pain as Gods' megaphone is a terrible instrument; it may lead to final and unrepented rebellion. But it gives the only opportunity the bad man can have for amendment. It removes the veil; it plants the flag of truth within the fortress of a rebel soul. *(The Problem of Pain*, pg.95)

When we do become aware of our own wickedness and realize our great dependence on the Lord, we find that God is patient and forgiving, and wants to welcome us back. C.S. Lewis comments about this principle:

I call this a Divine humility because it is a poor thing to strike our colours to God when the ship is going down under us; a poor thing to come to Him as a last resort, to offer up "our own" when it is no longer worth keeping. If God were proud He would hardly have us on such terms; but He is not proud, He stoops to conquer, He will have us even though we have shown that we prefer everything else to Him, and come to Him because there is "nothing better" now to be had. The same humility is shown by all those Divine appeals to our fears which trouble high-minded readers of scripture. It is hardly complimentary to God that we should choose Him as an alternative to Hell: yet even this He accepts. The creature's illusion of self-sufficiency must, for the creature's sake, be shattered; and by trouble or fear of trouble on earth, by crude fear of the eternal flames, God shatters it "unmindful of His glory's diminution."[300]

Let us take one line from above and steer into something rather profound, that most of us prefer to ignore. He says, "The creature's illusion of self-sufficiency must, for the creature's sake, be shattered…" Brigham Young understood this well. He taught:

> Take courage, brethren…plow your land and sow wheat, plant your potatoes. It is our duty to preach the Gospel, gather Israel, pay our tithing and build temples. The worst fear I have about this people is that they will get rich in this country, forget God and His people, wax fat, and kick themselves out of the Church and go to hell. This people will stand mobbing, robbing, poverty, and all manner of persecution and be true. But my greatest fear is that they cannot stand wealth.[301]

Here is a tough dilemma. We all seek security. Often it is in the form of a better paying job, a larger home, another car, etc. But it is these very things that put us in danger of what Brigham and C.S. are talking about. Why is it that riches are more dangerous to us than mobbing, robbing, poverty and persecutions? Because within these there is pain — physical and spiritual — which causes us to seek out the Lord. Ease and prosperity lull us into the delusion that we've got a pretty good handle on life just how it is, and it is at these moments that we cut ourselves off from God one little inch at a time.

In order for God to mold us into that celestial shape in which we belong, He must know us. And know us He does — more so than anyone else. He knows us like an artist knows his painting. In the following passage C.S. Lewis demonstrates a remarkable and touching understanding of our personal relationship with God:

If He had no use for all these differences, I do not see why He should have created more souls than one. Be sure that the ins and outs of your individuality are no mystery to Him; and one day they will no longer be a mystery to you. The mould in which a key is made would be a strange thing, if you had never seen a key: and the key itself a strange thing if you had never seen a lock.... For it is not humanity in the abstract that is to be saved, but you — you, the individual reader, John Stubbs or Janet Smith. Blessed and fortunate creature, your eyes shall behold Him and not another's.[302]

James E. Talmage wrote about this concept of our relationship with God, and how we lived with Him and were taught by Him. His words were:

Our Heavenly Father has a full knowledge of the nature and disposition of each of His children, a knowledge gained by long observation and experience in the past eternity of our primeval childhood; a knowledge compared with which that gained by earthly parents through mortal experience with their children is infinitesimally small. By reason of that surpassing knowledge, God reads the future of child and children, of men individually and of men collectively as communities and nations; He knows what each will do under given conditions, and sees the end from the beginning. His foreknowledge is based on intelligence and reason. He foresees the future as a state which naturally and surely will be; not as one which must be because He has arbitrarily willed that it shall be.[303]

Another point here — he mentions God's foreknowledge of our actions. He knows us so thoroughly that He can't help but know what we will do under any set of circumstances. However, this does not interfere with our agency. Bruce R. McConkie wrote:

Predestination is a sectarian substitute for the true doctrine of foreordination. Just as Lucifer "sought to destroy the agency of man" in pre-existence (Moses 4:3), so through his ministers here he has taught a doctrine, based on scriptural distortions, of salvation and damnation without choice on the part of the individual. Predestination is the false doctrine that from all eternity God has ordered whatever comes to pass, having especial and particular reference to the salvation or damnation of souls. Some souls, according to this false concept, are irrevocably chosen for salvation, others for damnation; and there is said to be nothing any individual can do to escape his predestined inheritance in heaven or in hell as the case may be.[304]

C.S. Lewis shares a similar belief. He said:

> [God] does not foresee the humans making their free contribu-
> tions in a future, but sees them doing so in His unbounded Now.
> And obviously to watch a man doing something is not to make
> him do it.[305]

Another truth is hit upon by C.S. Lewis, and that is that we are
saved individually — not as a nation or a church. In *The Screwtape
Letters*, Screwtape, a master tempter, writes to his nephew
Wormwood, a junior tempter, the following idea:

> I mean the delusion that the fate of nations is *in itself* more
> important than that of individual souls. The overthrow of free
> peoples and the multiplication of slave states are for us a means
> (besides, of course, being fun); but the real end is the destruction
> of individuals. For only individuals can be saved or damned, can
> become sons of the Enemy or food for us.[306]

The year C.S. Lewis died, Elder El Ray L. Christiansen spoke the
following words in conference on this same subject:

> Now, while we see the Church moving on unfalteringly
> toward its decreed destiny, we must remember that salvation for
> each of us must be worked out on an individual basis.[307]

And just as salvation is individual, so also are our trials and our
subsequent joys. After his harrowing experience, Alma said, "And
oh, what joy, and what marvelous light I did behold; yea, my soul
was filled with joy as exceeding as was my pain!"[308] Spencer W.
Kimball offered a perspective on individual joy — the end purpose
in our relationship with God:

> ...I once went to the top of a mountain which I had never
> climbed before. And from those heights I saw a beautiful valley I
> had never seen before. I gasped at the beauty of the scene. The far-
> reaching valley in the distance, and the mountains beyond. I saw
> the homes shimmering in the sun and the metal barns reflecting
> the light. I saw the clumps of trees and orchards and groves and
> vineyards. I saw the farms that raise alfalfa, grain, and cotton and
> I gasped at the sheer beauty of them. I imagine that it might be
> just a little taste of what one might see after emerging through the
> veil. "Eye hath not seen, nor ear heard, neither have entered into
> the heart of man, the things which God hath prepared for them
> that love him." (1 Corinthians 2:9)[309]

God is love, and if we want to become like God, we must become love too. Love is such an integral part of the gospel, and such a guiding force in the universe, that unless we learn to develop the pure love of Christ, as Paul says, we are nothing. C.S. Lewis, in *The Problem of Pain*, wrote about the love of God in the following way:

> You asked for a loving God: you have one. The great spirit you so lightly invoked, the 'lord of terrible aspect,' is present: not a senile benevolence that drowsily wishes you to be happy in your own way, not the cold philanthropy of a conscientious magistrate, not the care of a host who feels responsible for the comfort of his guests, but the consuming fire Himself, the Love that made the worlds, persistent as the artist's love for his work and despotic as a man's love for a dog, provident and venerable as a father's love for a child, jealous, inexorable, exacting as love between the sexes. (*The Problem of Pain*, pg.46)

He expounds further about this kind of love:

> ...to be loved by God, not merely pitied, but delighted in as an artist delights in his work or a father in a son — it seems impossible, a weight or burden of glory which our thoughts can hardly sustain. But so it is.[310]

Again, he hits the nail on the head. Compare the above statement with a revelation from the Lord to Joseph Smith:

> These things remain to overcome through patience, that such may receive a more exceeding and eternal weight of glory, otherwise, a greater condemnation. Amen.[311]

That is the serious business of the Lord — helping us, his children, become the types of creatures that experience a "weight" of glory. How magnificent an idea this is! Still it is a constant and lifelong struggle to become what He is trying to make us. But, many times people do not want, of course, to be molded at all. They don't want to be governed, and think, perhaps, that their way is better. Consider these words by C.S. Lewis:

> And it is no use either saying that if there is a God of that sort — an impersonal absolute goodness — then you do not like Him and are not going to bother about Him. For the trouble is that one part of you is on His side and really agrees with His disapproval of human greed and trickery and exploitation. You may want Him

to make an exception in your own case, to let you off this one time; but you know at bottom that unless the power behind the world really and unalterably detests that sort of behaviour, that He cannot be good. On the other hand, we know that if there does exist an absolute goodness it must hate most of what we do. That is the terrible fix we are in. If the universe is not governed by an absolute goodness, then all our efforts are in the long run hopeless. But if it is, then we are making ourselves enemies to that goodness every day, and are not in the least likely to be any better tomorrow, and so our case is hopeless again. We cannot do without it, and we cannot do with it. God is the only comfort, He is also the supreme terror: the thing we most need and the thing we most want to hide from. He is our only possible ally, and we have made ourselves His enemies. Some people talk as if meeting the gaze of absolute goodness would be fun. They need to think again. They are still only playing with religion. Goodness is either the great safety or the great danger — according to the way you react to it.[312]

Each soul is born with the light of Christ within him or her. We all know, to some extent, what is right and what is wrong, yet we constantly try to rationalize ourselves out of that and into our own agenda, whatever it may be. Still, our conscience is always there, trying to whisper what will make us right, minute by minute, with the Lord. Marion D. Hanks said this about our conscience:

Is good conscience important? It is a prize beyond expression! And conscience is more than a local standard or the accumulation of the morals and traditions of a community or a society or a generation. Whatever else it is, it is the voice of God speaking to us, inspiring moral obligation. Washington called it "that little spark of celestial fire." It is true that we can desensitize our conscience, as it were. In *The Book of Mormon* we read of a group to whom God had spoken "in a still small voice, but ye were past feeling." (1 Ne. 17:45) It is also said that there are those who have become "dead as to things pertaining unto righteousness." As we can desensitize a conscience, so to speak, so we can prepare ourselves better to hear the voice of the Lord by stripping off what the poet called the layers of "muddy vesture and decay," by ceasing to sin and learning to obey. There is the privilege of learning true values and living to them.[313]

Of this principle, C.S. Lewis said simply, "The more you obey your conscience, the more your conscience will demand of you." *(Mere Christianity)* That is a basic principle of the gospel. When we heed and follow the light and knowledge the Lord imparts to us, we are given more. When we heed less we are given less, and even have taken away what is already within us. Now think of this in relation to what God expects of us, and think about what C.S. Lewis believed on the matter. There is great wisdom in it, and his words echo the truth we have received through the restored gospel.

>...Now, once again, what God cares about is not exactly our actions, what He cares about is that we should be creatures of a certain kind or quality — the kind of creatures He intended us to be — creatures related to Himself in a certain way. I do not add "and related to one another in a certain way," because that is included: if you are right with Him you will inevitably be right with all your fellow-creatures, just as if all the spokes of a wheel are fitted rightly into the hub and the rim they are bound to be in the right positions to one another. And as long as man is thinking of God as an examiner who has set him a sort of paper to do, or as the opposite party in a sort of bargain — as long as he is thinking of claims and counterclaims between himself and God — he is not yet in the right relation to Him. He is misunderstanding what he is and what God is. And he cannot get into the right relation until he has discovered the fact of our bankruptcy.

>When I say "discovered," I mean really discovered: not simply said it in parrot-fashion. Of course, any child, if given a certain kind of religious education, will soon learn to say that we have nothing to offer to God that is not already His own and that we find ourselves failing to offer even that without keeping something back. But I am talking of really discovering this: really finding out by experience that it is true.

>Now we cannot, in that sense, discover our failure to keep God's law except by trying our very hardest (and then failing). Unless we really try, whatever we say there will always be at the back of our minds the idea that if we try harder next time we shall succeed in being completely good. Thus, in one sense, the road back to God is a road of moral effort, of trying harder and harder. But in another sense it is not trying that is ever going to bring us home. All this trying leads up to the vital moment at which you turn to God and say, "you must do this. I can't." Do not, I implore you, start asking yourselves, "Have I reached that moment?" Do not sit down and start with your own mind to see if it is coming along. That puts a man quite on the wrong track. When the most important things in our life happen we quite often do not know, at the moment, what is going on. A man does not always say to himself, "Hullo! I'm growing up."[314]

Also, compare his words about realizing our own nothingness and dependence upon God with those of King Benjamin:

And again I say unto you as I have said before, that as ye have come to the knowledge of the glory of God, or if ye have known of his goodness and have tasted of his love, and have received a remission of your sins, which causeth such exceedingly great joy in your souls, even so I would that ye should remember, and always retain in remembrance, the greatness of God, and your own nothingness, and his goodness and long-suffering towards you, unworthy creatures, and humble yourselves even in the depths of humility, calling on the name of the Lord daily, and standing steadfastly in the faith of that which is to come, which was spoken by the mouth of the angel.[315]

Again, compare this with the remarkable insights of C.S. Lewis:

Then comes another discovery. Every faculty you have, your power of thinking or of moving your limbs from moment to moment, is given you by God. If you devoted every moment of your whole life exclusively to His service you could not give Him anything that was not is a sense His own already. So that when we talk of a man doing anything for God or giving anything to God, I will tell you what it is really like. It is like a small child going to its father and saying, "Daddy, give me sixpence to buy you a birthday present." Of course, the father does, and he is pleased with the child's present. It is all very nice and proper, but only an idiot would think that the father is sixpence to the good on the transaction. When a man has made these two discoveries God can really get to work. It is after this that real life begins. The man is awake now. [316]

Much of what God requires of us is actually for our benefit and not His. When He asks for tithing, He does not need the money, but we need the blessings, the buildings, the temples, and the sacrifice. When He asks us to worship Him and praise Him, it is not because He needs it to make Him feel good, but in so doing we focus our affections and aspirations on the one source of eternal joy. When He asks us to keep the Sabbath day Holy, it is probably because we desperately need a frequent reminder that everything is really His, and so that we will have one entire day in seven to refocus our priorities on the fountain of living waters.

One last concept: To whom do our lives belong? C.S. Lewis was quite clear on this doctrine. He wrote:

They wanted, as we say, to "call their souls their own." But that means to live a lie, for our souls are not, in fact, our own. They wanted some corner in the universe of which they could say to God, "This is our business, not yours." But there is no such corner.[317]

To take this idea a bit further, C.S. Lewis wrote:

> Much of the modern resistance to chastity comes from men's belief that they "own" their bodies — those vast and perilous estates, pulsating with the energy that made the worlds, in which they find themselves without their consent and from which they are ejected at the pleasure of Another. *(Mere Christianity)*

That puts the whole thing in quite a different perspective, doesn't it? Elder Neal A. Maxwell taught about the dangerous "It's my life!" philosophy in these words:

> One of the last, subtle strongholds of selfishness is the natural feeling that we "own" ourselves. Of course, we are free to choose and are personally accountable. Yes, we have individuality. But those who have chosen to "come unto Christ" soon realize that they do not "own" themselves. Instead, they belong to Him! We are to become consecrated along with our gifts, our appointed days, and our very selves. Hence there is a stark difference between stubbornly "owning" oneself and submissively belonging to God. Clinging to the old self is a mark not of independence but of indulgence.[318]

Recall the basic and resounding doctrine spoken by Jesus himself: "He who loseth his life for my sake shall find it again." That is the only way! C.S. Lewis goes into a little more depth about the idea of us being "stewards" rather than "owners" of our lives. He used the terms "owners" and "tenants" as follows:

> But does it not make a great difference whether his ship is his own property or not? Does it not make a great difference whether I am, so to speak, the landlord of my own mind and body, or only a tenant, responsible to the real landlord? If somebody else made me, for his own purposes, then I shall have a lot of duties which I should not have if I simply belonged to myself. *(The Problem of Pain)*

He understood that our relationship with God is not merely a vital acquaintance, but that the relationship, in itself, is of the utmost importance to our eternal well being. He knew that if Satan could succeed in driving a wedge between us and Him, the war would be over. Here is another excerpt from *The Screwtape Letters*, from Uncle Screwtape to Wormwood:

You will say that these are very small sins; and doubtless, like all young tempters, you are anxious to be able to report spectacular wickedness. But do remember, the only thing that matters is the extent to which you separate the man from the Enemy. It does not matter how small the sins are, provided that their cumulative effect is to edge the man away from the Light and out into the Nothing. Murder is no better than cards if cards can do the trick. Indeed, the safest road to Hell is the gradual one — the gentle slope, soft underfoot, without sudden turning, without milestones, without signposts. *(The Screwtape Letters, pg.54)*

So eloquently stated, how the devil "leadeth them carefully down to hell." Think of all the things in the world today that effectively (and consistently) separate us from our Maker. C.S. Lewis had a true and concise picture of this doctrine. He said simply, "To be discontinuous from God as I am discontinuous from you would be annihilation." *(The Problem of Pain)* And so, spiritual death is, in a sense, annihilation. How thankful we must be that our Heavenly Father's arms are continuously outstretched for us. His offer is forever open: "Come unto me."

What Think Ye of Christ?

— Matthew 22:42

CHAPTER 22

What Thought He of Christ?

In our age of enlightened and modern thinking, many people, both religious and nonreligious, have denied the divinity of Jesus Christ. The war began in the premortal life between God and Satan and has continued down here. But the enemy is camouflaged and sophisticated. In the April 10, 1995 edition of *Time* magazine, the issue of the divinity of our Savior was analyzed. Compare some of the following ideas with those of C.S. Lewis. Apparently, even in his generation, the same bold ideas were present. *Time* reports:

> Last month, just in time for Lent, the rebel scholars of the self-appointed Bible tribunal called the Jesus Seminar gathered once again, this time to vote on the most explosive question of Christian faith: Did Jesus literally rise from the dead? That such a vote would even take place says a lot about current Bible scholarship; that the result, by an overwhelming majority, was to announce, No he did not, shows clearly the chasm that has opened between some professors of Scripture and the true-believing flock.

> ....The popular interest in miracles, it turns out, comes along just as a generation of Bible scholars is dedicated to disproving them. From both seminaries and secular institutions, scholars are drawing on science, archaeology and modern textual criticisms to write a chapter of Christianity that makes little mention of miracles except to reject them. They believe the teachings of Jesus are more important than the teachings about Jesus. In this book there is no virgin birth, no walking on water; the healings amount to parlor tricks, and the Resurrection never happened.

> "I don't think the Bible is literally true," says Bishop John Spong of the Episcopal diocese of Newark, New Jersey, answering a question scholars have tugged at for the past 200 years...There are a whole lot of literal concepts out of the Bible that have long ago been abandoned. I'd like to think Christianity is something that would appeal to people who are also well educated and who are modern people."

The modern skeptics analyze Scripture through the lenses of science, politics and literature. The rationalists study the medical impact of crucifixion and suggest perhaps it induced a deep coma from which Jesus might have revived. They search for evidence of a volcanic eruption that could have caused the Red Sea to part. Perhaps a comet swept across the Bethlehem skies, disguised as the Star in the East...But liberal theologians are prepared to reduce the role of Christ to that of a placebo: people's belief in his healing power was enough to cure ailments that were psychosomatic to begin with.

...A parallel line of argument holds that the Bible is made up simply of legends crafted by the Gospel writers to serve a political agenda in the early days of the church.

...The chief purveyor of this political revisionism is ex-priest John Dominic Crossan, a professor of biblical studies at Catholic De Paul University. In Crossan's view, the Gospel accounts are parables about power and authority in the new church..."Jesus was 'healing' people ideologically, saying the Kingdom of God is against this system."

...Yet liberals argue that it is not blasphemy to say the Resurrection never happened, because accounts of Christ's rising are meant metaphorically. In this view, one robs the Bible of its richness and poetry by insisting it should be read literally. Jesus was resurrected in the lives and dreams of his followers; the body of Christ is the church, not a reconstituted physical body. The Resurrection represents an explosion of power, a promise of salvation that does not depend on a literal belief in physical resurrection.

...The effort of moderate theologians to find new meanings in Scripture are burdened by the decrees of such groups as the Jesus Seminar, which seem determined to offend at all costs. The seminar is the invention of onetime Protestant clergyman Robert W. Funk, who now runs a Bible think tank, the Westar Institute. Since the mainstream press rarely covers the esoterica of New Testament criticism, he set an irresistible trap: he would gather "eminent" scholars, and they would put the events in the Bible to a vote. He passes around a white plastic container, and each scholar drops in a colored marble: black if he or she is certain the event was fabricated, gray if it probably was, pink if it might actually have occurred, red if it certainly did.

In recent years, the Jesus Seminar weighed Christ's actual words as reported in the Gospels, and agreed that in most cases he never said them. Last fall they considered the Virgin Birth, and 96% agreed it never happened. And last month, just in time for Easter, they took up the subject of the Resurrection. The invitation to reporters promised that the experts "will be drilling close to the nerve of the Christian faith."

Close indeed. The Bible's account of the event that rests at the heart of Christian faith, they concluded, is a poetic rendering of a devout wish but certainly not an authentic record. Crossan, who is co-chairman of the seminar with Funk, argues it this way: since the Crucifixion was conducted by Roman soldiers, he reckons, Jesus' body was most likely left on the Cross or tossed into a shallow grave to be eaten by scavenger dogs, crows or other wild beasts. As for Jesus' family and followers, depicted in the Bible as conducting a decent burial of the body according to Jewish law, "as far as I can see, they ran," Crossan says.[319]

The above commentary hardly merits discussion except to note that it is apparent that the arch-deceiver is alive and well in the world. There have always been anti-Christs, even in sheep's clothing. C.S. Lewis strongly believed in the reality and divinity of Christ. When you read his words on the subject, many times you may think he is bearing his testimony. He wrote:

There was a man born among these Jews who claimed to be, or to be the son of, or to be "one with," the Something which is at once the awful haunter of nature and giver of the moral law. The claim is so shocking — a paradox, and even a horror, which we may easily be lulled into taking too lightly — that only two views of this man are possible. Either he was a raving lunatic of an unusually abominable type, or else He was, and is, precisely what He said. There is no middle way. If the records make the first hypothesis unacceptable, you must submit to the second. And if you do that, all else that is claimed by Christians becomes credible — that this Man, having been killed, was yet alive, and that His death, in some manner incomprehensible to human thought, has effected a real change in our relations to the "awful" and "right-eous" Lord, and a change in our favour...Christianity is not the conclusion of a philosophical debate on the origins of the universe: it is a catastrophic historical event following on the long spiritual preparation of humanity...[320]

There was indeed a mortal Messiah who was resurrected, and He lives today. All the philosophizing and analyzing of history, science, or culture cannot change that fact — and facts are stubborn things. Ezra Taft Benson spoke the following:

God help us to live the gospel. I testify to you that God has again spoken from the heavens. The heavens are not sealed. The vision of

God the Father and the Son to the boy prophet did in very deed occur. God lives. Jesus is the Christ, the Redeemer of the world, not just a great moral teacher, as much of the Christian world is claiming, but the Savior of mankind, the very Son of God.[321]

I have read the words of educated people, experts, and theologians as they meandered through their hazy ideas about the Bible being partly myth, about truth being relative, and even about Jesus Christ being less than He said He was. But I have also heard with my own ears living apostles of the Lord Jesus Christ bear testimony of Him so powerfully that I knew that they knew. Oliver Cowdery once penned these great words:

Man may deceive his fellow-men, deception may follow deception, and the children of the wicked one may have power to seduce the foolish and untaught, till naught but fiction feeds the many, and the fruit of falsehood carries in its current the giddy to the grave; but one touch with the finger of his love, yes, one ray of glory from the upper world, or one word from the mouth of the Savior, from the bosom of eternity, strikes it all into insignificance, and blots it forever from the mind.[322]

False doctrines come and go, but the truth remains forever. Now let us examine more of what C.S. Lewis thought of Christ. He said:

I am here to prevent anyone saying the really foolish thing that people often say about Him: "I'm ready to accept Jesus as a great moral teacher, but I don't accept His claim to be God." That is the one thing we must not say. A man who was merely a man and said the sort of things Jesus said would not be a great moral teacher. He would either be a lunatic — on a level with the man who says he is a poached egg — or else he would be the Devil of Hell. You must make your choice. Either this man was, and is, the Son of God: or else a madman or something worse. You can shut Him up for a fool, you can spit at Him and kill Him as a demon; or you can fall at His feet and call Him Lord and God. But let us not come with any patronizing nonsense about His being a great human teacher. He has not left that open to us. He did not intend to.[323]

Since the days of Adam, nearly every prophet prophesied of the coming of the Savior. When He did come, he healed the sick, raised the dead, and died for the sins of the world. In 1820, He and His Father came to Joseph Smith to usher in the long awaited dispensation of the fullness of times. He was a great moral teacher, but He was so much more. Joseph Fielding Smith addressed the issue this way:

Throughout the length of the land the cry has been raised that churches are empty; pulpits are being deserted; houses of worship are for sale, or being transformed into buildings for other purposes. Ministers who profess to be Christians stand before their congregations without a blush and confess that they have no faith in the divine mission of Jesus Christ. They accept him merely as a great moral and ethical teacher, but not as the Only Begotten Son of God.[324]

C.S. Lewis stated:

For when you get down to it, is not the popular idea of Christianity simply this: that Jesus Christ was a great moral teacher and that if only we took his advice we might be able to establish a better social order and avoid another war? Now, mind you, that is quite true. But it tells you much less than the whole truth about Christianity and it has no practical importance at all. Then comes the real shock. Among these Jews there suddenly turns up a man who goes about talking as if He was God. He claims to forgive sins. He says He has always existed. He says He is coming to judge the world at the end of time. Now let us get this clear. Among Pantheists, like the Indians, anyone might say that he was a part of God, or one with God: there would be nothing very odd about it. But this man, since He was a Jew, could not mean that kind of God. God, in their language, meant the Being outside the world Who had made it and was infinitely different from anything else. And when you have grasped that, you will see that what this man said was, quite simply, the most shocking thing that has ever been uttered by human lips.[325]

If truth is nothing more than comfort, or our best guess at any given time, how can we pretend that there is any truth at all? Jesus proclaimed that He was the son of God. If we have a shred of honesty then we must jump entirely on one side of the fence or the other, and not mill around in the limbo of this pretended "re-evaluation" of the doctrines of Christ. God has not given us the prerogative of voting on truth. The only voting to be done is over the issue of whether we are for God or against Him. That, He has left entirely up to us. C.S. Lewis was not sucked into the quagmire of the philosophical haze regarding whether or not Jesus is in every sense the literal anointed One. He wrote:

Why are many people prepared in advance to maintain that, whatever else God may be, He is not the concrete, living, willing, and acting God of Christian theology? I think the reason is as follows. Let us suppose a mystical limpet, a sage among limpets, who (rapt in vision) catches a glimpse of what Man is like. In reporting it to his disciples, who have some vision themselves (though less than he) he will have to use many negatives. He will have to tell them that Man has no shell, is not attached to a rock, is not surrounded by water. And his disciples, having a little vision of their own to help them, do get some idea of Man. But then there come erudite limpets, limpets who write histories of philosophy and give lectures on comparative religion, and who have never had any vision of their own. What they get out of the prophetic limpet's words is simply and solely the negatives. From these, uncorrected by any positive insight, they build up a picture of Man a sort of amorphous jelly (he has no shell) existing nowhere in particular (he is not attached to a rock) and never taking nourishment (there is no water to drift in towards him). And having a traditional reverence for Man they conclude that to be a famished jelly in a dimensionless void is the supreme mode of existence, and reject as crude, materialistic superstition any doctrine which would attribute to Man a definite shape, a structure, and organs.[326]

In his closing remark from the above excerpt, he takes a doctrinal leap away from the general consensus of modern Christianity, saying that God has a definite shape, structure, and organs — in other words, a literal, resurrected, physical body. He stands singularly with the Latter-day Saints. Compare his thoughts with those of Ezra Taft Benson:

> Several years ago, a number of prominent theologians were asked the question, What do you think of Jesus? Their replies startled many professed Christians. One asserted that a "true Christian" must reject the Resurrection. Another admitted that New Testament scholars were so divided on the question that one cannot say anything certain about the historical Jesus. Another scholar and teacher of Jesuit priests explained, "It is difficult to say in our age what the divinity of Jesus can mean. We are groping now for a way to express it — we just don't know."[327]

And again from Ezra Taft Benson:

> From the time of Christ's heaven-heralded birth, heresies have crept into Christianity intended to dilute or undermine the pure doctrines of the gospel. These heresies, by and large, are sponsored by the philosophies of men and, in many instances, advocated by so-called Christian scholars. Their intent is to make Christianity more palatable, more reasonable, and so they attempt to humanize Jesus and give natural explanations to those things which are divine.[328]

The following observation of C.S. Lewis is interesting — it is sure to make an impression on you:

> God, from above or outside or all round, contains the whole line, and sees it all. He says again 'I am the begotten of the One God, before Abraham was, I am,' and remember that the words 'I am' were in Hebrew. They were the name of God, which must not be spoken by any human being, the name which it was death to utter...
>
> If you had gone to Buddha and asked him, 'Are you the son of Bramah?' he would have said, 'My son, you are still in the vale of illusion.' If you had gone to Socrates and asked, 'Are you Zeus?' he would have laughed at you. If you had gone to Mohammed and asked, 'Are you Allah?' he would first have rent his clothes and then cut your head off. If you had asked Confucius, 'Are you Heaven?' I think he would have probably replied, 'Remarks which are not in accordance with nature are in bad taste.' The idea of a great moral teacher saying what Christ said is out of the question. In my opinion, the only person who can say that sort of thing is either God or a complete lunatic suffering from that form of delusion which undermines the whole mind of man...He was never regarded as a mere moral teacher. He did not produce that effect on any of the people who actually met Him. He produced mainly three effects — Hatred — Terror — Adoration. There was no trace of people expressing mild approval.[329]

The scriptures say that we are to become the children of Christ. What does this mean? C.S. Lewis offers an interesting view:

> Now the point in Christianity which gives us the greatest shock is the statement that by attaching ourselves to Christ, we can "become Sons of God." One asks "Aren't we Sons of God already? Surely the fatherhood of God is one of the main Christian ideas?" Well, in a certain sense, no doubt we are sons of God already. I mean, God has brought us into existence and loves us and looks after us, and in that way is like a father. But when the Bible talks of our "becoming" Sons of God, obviously it must mean something different. And that brings us up against the very centre of Theology.
>
> One of the creeds says that Christ is the Son of God "begotten, not created;" and it adds "begotten by his Father before all worlds." Will you please get it quite clear that this has nothing to do with the fact that when Christ was born on earth as a man, that man was the son of a virgin? We are not now thinking about the Virgin Birth. We are thinking about something that happened before Nature was created at all, before time began.[330]

From Mosiah 5:7 we read:

> And now, because of the covenant which ye have made ye shall be called the children of Christ, his sons, and his daughters; for behold, this day he hath spiritually begotten you; for ye say that your hearts are changed through faith on his name; therefore, ye are born of him and have become his sons and his daughters.

One final point is that of the Second Coming. C.S. Lewis wrote this on the subject:

> The idea which...shuts out the Second coming from our minds, the idea of the world slowly ripening to perfection, is a myth, not a generalization from experience. And it is anything which distracts us from our real duties and our real interest. It is our attempt to guess the plot of a drama in which we are the characters. But how can the characters in a play guess the plot? We are not the playwright, we are not the producer, we are not even the audience. We are on the stage. To play well the scenes in which we are 'on' concerns us much more than to guess about the scenes that follow it.[331]

Here is another thought of his, contrary to the earth "ripening to perfection:"

> There are those, too, who claim that the gospel is old-fashioned; that men through scientific development are becoming more and more self-sufficient and need not rely on God. Others argue that the gospel is too restrictive, that it takes away our liberty, and that we cannot enjoy the advantages of a broad education, accept scientific truths, and participate in worthwhile community activities.[332]

He had a strong grasp on the true idea of the Second Coming in that it will come like "a thief in the night." Also, he discounts the idea of "the world slowly ripening to perfection." This idea was started and developed by the modernists, but few people really buy into it, except in a sort of wishful-thinking way. While they say the world is ripening to perfection, the Lord says the world is "ripening in iniquity."

I believe C.S. Lewis had a testimony of the Lord Jesus Christ. He knew of His divinity, the importance of His mission, and the truthfulness of His words. He would probably have said of the Lord, as did Peter, "Thou art the Christ, the son of the living God."[333] C.S. Lewis must have been, to some degree, a humble follower of Christ, because it is certainly not the fashionable thing (nor ever has been) to take Him literally — to take His words at face value and courageously live by them. Yes, I think C.S. Lewis knew the Lord in his own way, and perhaps more than we know.

Appendix of Quotes

1 *Mere Christianity*, vi
2 *The Problem of Pain*
3 Lewis, C.S. *Mere Christianity*. Collier Books. Macmillan Publishing Company, 1952. pg.13
4 *Gospel Ideals*, pg.31
5 *The Magician's Nephew*, ch.10
6 Man or Rabbit?
7 Lewis, C.S. *Mere Christianity*. Collier Books. Macmillan Publishing Company, 1952. pg.167
8 D&C 1:31
9 Lewis, C.S. *The Problem of Pain*. New York: The Macmillan Company, 1962. pg.48
10 Neal A. Maxwell, *We Will Prove Them Herewith*, pg.15
11 Lewis, C.S. *The Problem of Pain*. New York: The Macmillan Company, 1962. pg.115
12 Lewis, C.S. *The Problem of Pain*. New York: The Macmillan Company, 1962. pg.96
13 D&C 58:2
14 Bruce R. McConkie, *Mormon Doctrine*, pg.809 TRIBULATIONS
15 D&C 128:24
16 Lewis, C.S. *The Problem of Pain*. New York: The Macmillan Company, 1962. pg.105
17 D&C 43:25
18 Bruce R. McConkie, *Mormon Doctrine*, pg.162
19 Lewis, C.S. *Mere Christianity*. Collier Books. Macmillan Publishing Company, 1952. pg.124.
20 Teachings of Ezra Taft Benson, pg.330 ("Power Through Service," *Millennial Star* 118 [9 October 1956]: 298).
21 Lewis, C.S. *Mere Christianity*. Collier Books. Macmillan Publishing Company, 1952. pg.153.
22 Ibid. pg.160.
23 'Christianity and Culture,' Christian Reflections
24 *The Problem of Pain*
25 *Lectures on Faith*, Lecture 6, pg.58
26 Lewis, C.S. *Mere Christianity*. Collier Books. Macmillan Publishing Company, 1952. pg.148
27 Ibid. pg.157
28 Moses 1:39
29 Bruce R. McConkie, Doctrinal New Testament Commentary, Vol.1, pg.183-184 *(Mormon Doctrine, pp. 566-568.)*
30 Lewis, C.S. *The Problem of Pain*. New York: The Macmillan Company, 1962. pg.61
31 Mosiah 13:29
32 Spencer W. Kimball, *The Miracle of Forgiveness*, pg.19
33 D&C 88:40
34 Teachings of the Prophet Joseph Smith, Section Five 1842-43 p.280
35 Teachings of Ezra Taft Benson, pg.79
36 Mark E. Petersen, *The Way to Peace*, pg.152
37 Ibid. pg.197
38 Neal A. Maxwell, *Men and Women of Christ*, pg.71
39 Neal A. Maxwell, *We Will Prove Them Herewith*, pg.114
40 *Serious Call*, Chapter 2
41 Matthew 6:33

42 Lewis, C.S. *Mere Christianity*. Collier Books. Macmillan Publishing Company, 1952. pg.62

43 *Collected Works of Hugh Nibley*, Vol.9, ch.8, pg.211

44 *Discourses of Brigham Young*, p.180-181

45 2 Nephi 28:21

46 *Discourses of Brigham Young*, pg.306 (7:135)

47 Alma 4:8

48 Lewis, C.S. *The Screwtape Letters*. Collier Books — Macmillan Publishing Company. NEW YORK, 1961. pg.49

49 *Teachings of Ezra Taft Benson*, pg.553-554

50 Lewis, C.S. *The Screwtape Letters*. Collier Books — Macmillan Publishing Company. NEW YORK, 1961. pg.133

51 Teachings of Ezra Taft Benson, pg.350

52 David O. McKay, *Gospel Ideals*, pg.40

53 Lewis, C.S. *The Screwtape Letters*. Collier Books — Macmillan Publishing Company. NEW YORK, 1961. pg.164

54 Neal A. Maxwell, *We Talk of Christ*, pg.63

55 Lewis, C.S. *The Screwtape Letters*. Collier Books — Macmillan Publishing Company. NEW YORK, 1961. pg.22

56 Lewis, C.S. *Mere Christianity*. Collier Books. Macmillan Publishing Company, 1952. pg.72

57 *Reflections on the Psalms*, ch.3

58 Marion G. Romney, Conference Report, October 1968, pg.68

59 *Reflections on the Psalms*, ch.3

60 Ibid.

61 D&C 82:3

62 *Letters of C.S. Lewis* (20 Dec. 1961)

63 Lewis, C.S. *Mere Christianity*. Collier Books. Macmillan Publishing Company, 1952. pg.166

64 *Teachings of the Prophet Joseph Smith*, Section Six 1843-44 p.358

65 Lewis, C.S. *Mere Christianity*. Collier Books. Macmillan Publishing Company, 1952. pg.149

66 Matthew 26:41

67 Lewis, C.S. *The Screwtape Letters*. Collier Books — Macmillan Publishing Company. NEW YORK, 1961. pg.41

68 *Answers to Questions on Christianity*

69 D&C 88:22-24

70 Lewis, C.S. *The Problem of Pain*. New York: The Macmillan Company, 1962. pg.150

71 D&C 130:11

72 Lewis, C.S. *Mere Christianity*. Collier Books. Macmillan Publishing Company, 1952. pg.55

73 Ibid. pg.64

74 D&C 58:27

75 Lewis, C.S. *Mere Christianity*. Collier Books. Macmillan Publishing Company, 1952. pg.61

76 *Transposition and Other Addresses*, ch.2

77 Lewis, C.S. *The Problem of Pain*. New York: The Macmillan Company, 1962. pg.111

78 Ibid. pg.67-8

79 *The Weight of Glory*

80 Ether 12:39

81 John 15:13

82 Lewis, C.S. *The Problem of Pain*. New York: The Macmillan Company, 1962. pg.102

83 Bruce R. McConkie, *Mormon Doctrine*, pg.469 MARTYRDOM

[84] Bruce R. McConkie, *Mormon Doctrine*, pg.470 MARTYRDOM
[85] Lewis, C.S. *Mere Christianity*. Collier Books. Macmillan Publishing Company, 1952. pg.115
[86] Ibid. pg.128
[87] Dallin H. Oaks, *Pure in Heart*, pg.112
[88] *The Silver Chair*, ch.2
[89] Lewis, C.S. *The Problem of Pain*. New York: The Macmillan Company, 1962. pg.13-14
[90] Neal A. Maxwell, *Not My Will, But Thine*, pg.41
[91] *Encounter with Light*
[92] Lewis, C.S. *Mere Christianity*. Collier Books. Macmillan Publishing Company, 1952. pg.168
[93] Ibid. 1952. pg.55
[94] *Teachings of Ezra Taft Benson*, pg.600 (The Red Carpet, p. 102.)
[95] *Teachings of Ezra Taft Benson*, pg.617
[96] Lewis, C.S. *The Screwtape Letters*. Collier Books — Macmillan Publishing Company. NEW YORK, 1961. pg.12
[97] Ibid. pg.14
[98] Dallin H. Oaks, *Pure in Heart*, pg.142
[99] Mark E. Petersen, *The Way to Peace*, pg.305
[100] *The Allegory of Love*, ch.7, sec. 3
[101] 'Petitionary Prayer,' Christian Reflections
[102] *Letters of C.S. Lewis*
[103] *Letters to Malcolm*, ch.6
[104] Lewis, C.S. *The Screwtape Letters*, ch.27, Collier Books — Macmillan Publishing Company. NEW YORK, 1961
[105] *A Grief Observed*, ch.3
[106] D&C 5:14
[107] Alma 12:24
[108] Lewis, C.S. *Mere Christianity*. Collier Books. Macmillan Publishing Company, 1952. pg.50-51
[109] 2 Timothy 4:7
[110] Bruce R. McConkie, *Mormon Doctrine*, pg.839 WISDOM OF THE WORLD
[111] *They Asked for a Pater*, ch.9
[112] Bruce R. McConkie, *Mormon Doctrine*, pg.729
[113] *The Last Battle*, ch.9
[114] Neal A. Maxwell, *For the Power Is in Them*, pg.49
[115] Neal A. Maxwell, *Look Back at Sodom*, Introduction
[116] Lewis, C.S. *The Problem of Pain*. New York: The Macmillan Company, 1962. pg.57
[117] Ibid
[118] Lewis, C.S. *The Problem of Pain*. New York: The Macmillan Company, 1962. pg.85
[119] Lewis, C.S. *Mere Christianity*. Collier Books. Macmillan Publishing Company, 1952. pg.66
[120] Hugh B. Brown, Conference Report, April 1958, pg.109
[121] *Teachings of Ezra Taft Benson*, pg.307
[122] *Transposition and Other Addresses*
[123] Lewis, C.S. *Mere Christianity*. Collier Books. Macmillan Publishing Company, 1952. pg.78-9
[124] Teachings of Ezra Taft Benson, pg.222 (CR April 1986, *Ensign* 16 [May 1986]: 45.)
[125] Bruce R. McConkie, *Mormon Doctrine*, p.726 SIGNS OF THE TIMES
[126] Lewis, C.S. *Mere Christianity*. Collier Books. Macmillan Publishing Company, 1952. pg.115
[127] 2 Nephi 28:8

[128] Dallin H. Oaks, *Pure in Heart*, pg.84

[129] LeGrand Richards, Conference Report, October 1965, pg.86-87 (Quoted by George Q. Cannon, Life of Joseph Smith the Prophet, 1958 ed., p.345.)

[130] Lewis, C.S. *The Screwtape Letters*. Collier Books — Macmillan Publishing Company. NEW YORK, 1961. pg.8

[131] Teachings of Ezra Taft Benson, pg.303 ("Your Charge: To Increase in Wisdom and Favor with God and Man," *New Era* 9 [September 1979]: 40.)

[132] Lewis, C.S. *The Screwtape Letters*. Collier Books — Macmillan Publishing Company. NEW YORK, 1961. pg.128

[133] Ibid. pg.10

[134] Lewis, C.S. *Mere Christianity*. Collier Books. Macmillan Publishing Company, 1952. pg.120

[135] Lewis, C.S. *The Screwtape Letters*. Collier Books — Macmillan Publishing Company. NEW YORK, 1961. pg.91

[136] Ezra Taft Benson, *Improvement Era*, December 1970, pg.49

[137] Lewis, C.S. *The Screwtape Letters*. Collier Books — Macmillan Publishing Company. NEW YORK, 1961. pg.129

[138] *Miracles*, ch.10

[139] *Letters of C.S. Lewis* (25 May 1962)

[140] Lewis, C.S. *Mere Christianity*. Collier Books. Macmillan Publishing Company, 1952. bk 2, ch.5

[141] *Letters of C.S. Lewis*

[142] Mark E. Petersen, *The Way to Peace*, pg.117

[143] Neal A. Maxwell, *Things As They Really Are*, pg.37

[144] Mark E. Petersen, Conference Report, April 1969, pg.65

[145] Neal A. Maxwell, *Things As They Really Are*, pg.1-2

[146] Paul H. Dunn, Conference Report, April 1969, pg.149

[147] Neal A. Maxwell, *Even As I Am*, pg.43-44

[148] *Encounter with Light*

[149] Lewis, C.S. *Mere Christianity*. Collier Books. Macmillan Publishing Company, 1952. bk 3, ch.11

[150] Ibid. pg.104

[151] Ibid. pg.67

[152] Mosiah 4:21

[153] Lewis, C.S. *Mere Christianity*. Collier Books. Macmillan Publishing Company, 1952. pg.87

[154] *Discourses of Brigham Young*, pg.198

[155] Lewis, C.S. *Mere Christianity*. Collier Books. Macmillan Publishing Company, 1952. pg.65-66

[156] Bruce R. McConkie, *The Promised Messiah*, pg.553

[157] Neal A. Maxwell, *Not My Will, But Thine*, pg.41

[158] Lewis, C.S. *The Problem of Pain*. New York: The Macmillan Company, 1962. pg.33-4

[159] Neal A. Maxwell, *Not My Will, But Thine*, pg.91

[160] D&C 101:78

[161] Lewis, C.S. *The Problem of Pain*. New York: The Macmillan Company, 1962. pg.71

[162] Lewis, C.S. *Mere Christianity*. Collier Books. Macmillan Publishing Company, 1952. pg.37-38

[163] Ibid.

[164] Neal A. Maxwell, *Men and Women of Christ*, pg.113

[165] Lewis, C.S. *The Problem of Pain*. New York: The Macmillan Company, 1962. pg.89

[166] Lewis, C.S. *Mere Christianity*. Collier Books. Macmillan Publishing Company, 1952. pg.38

[167] Lewis, C.S. *The Problem of Pain*. New York: The Macmillan Company, 1962. pg.120-3

[168] *The Great Divorce*, ch.13

[169] Lewis, C.S. *Mere Christianity*. Collier Books. Macmillan Publishing Company, 1952. pg.102

[170] *Mere Christianity*, bk 2, ch.5

[171] 'The Humanitarian Theory of Punishment,' Res Judicatae (June 1953)

[172] D&C 88:33

[173] Bruce R. McConkie, *Mormon Doctrine*, pg.93 BOASTING

[174] Dallin H. Oaks, *Pure in Heart*, pg.95

[175] *The Screwtape Letters*, pg.81

[176] *Letters of C.S. Lewis* (18 February 1954)

[177] Lewis, C.S. *Mere Christianity*. Collier Books. Macmillan Publishing Company, 1952. pg.104

[178] Neal A. Maxwell, *The Smallest Part*, pg.36

[179] *A Grief Observed*, ch.4

[180] *Teachings of Spencer W. Kimball*, pg.30

[181] Lewis, C.S. *The Problem of Pain*. New York: The Macmillan Company, 1962. pg.53-4

[182] *Teachings of Lorenzo Snow*, pg.48-49 (May 1884, BLS, p.487)

[183] Lewis, C.S. *The Problem of Pain*. New York: The Macmillan Company, 1962. pg.144-5

[184] *The Great Divorce*

[185] *Transposition and Other Addresses*, ch.4

[186] *Letters to Malcolm*, ch.14

[187] James E. Talmage, *Jesus the Christ*, ch.32, pg.572-573

[188] Lewis, C.S. *Mere Christianity*. Collier Books. Macmillan Publishing Company, 1952. pg.38-9

[189] Lewis, C.S. *The Problem of Pain*. New York: The Macmillan Company, 1962. pg.126-7

[190] *The Great Divorce*, ch.9

[191] Lewis, C.S. *The Problem of Pain*. New York: The Macmillan Company, 1962. pg.127-8

[192] *The Great Divorce*, ch.9

[193] Ibid.

[194] Moses 7:37

[195] Lewis, C.S. *The Problem of Pain*. New York: The Macmillan Company, 1962. pg.152-3

[196] Lewis, C.S. *Mere Christianity*. Collier Books. Macmillan Publishing Company, 1952. pg.73

[197] Lewis, C.S. *The Screwtape Letters*. Collier Books — Macmillan Publishing Company. NEW YORK, 1961. pg.vii (preface).

[198] Ibid. pg.ix (preface)

[199] Bruce R. McConkie, *Mormon Doctrine*, pg.502

[200] Lewis, C.S. *The Screwtape Letters*. Collier Books — Macmillan Publishing Company. NEW YORK, 1961. pg.87

[201] Ibid. pg.149

[202] D&C 45:7

[203] Lewis, C.S. *The Screwtape Letters*. Collier Books — Macmillan Publishing Company. NEW YORK, 1961. pg.98-9

[204] *Discourses of Brigham Young*, pg.242-243 (9:244.)

[205] Lewis, C.S. *The Screwtape Letters*. Collier Books — Macmillan Publishing Company. NEW YORK, 1961. pg.102-3

[206] Lewis, C.S. *Mere Christianity*. Collier Books. Macmillan Publishing Company, 1952. pg.36

[207] 'The Trouble with "X,"' Bristol Diocesan Gazette (August 1948)

[208] *The Great Divorce*

[209] Preface to *The Great Divorce*

[210] Lewis, C.S. *Mere Christianity*. Collier Books. Macmillan Publishing Company, 1952. pg.83

[211] Lewis, C.S. *Mere Christianity*. Collier Books. Macmillan Publishing Company, 1952. pg.84-85

[212] Ibid. pg.85

[213] Lewis, C.S. *The Screwtape Letters*. Collier Books — Macmillan Publishing Company. NEW YORK, 1961. pg.32-33

[214] *Collected Works of Hugh Nibley*, Vol.9, ch.2, pg.54

[215] *The Teachings of Spencer W. Kimball*, pg.35

[216] Lewis, C.S. *Mere Christianity*. Collier Books. Macmillan Publishing Company, 1952. pg.36.

[217] Lewis, C.S. *The Screwtape Letters*. Collier Books — Macmillan Publishing Company. NEW YORK, 1961. pg.viii (preface)

[218] *The Problem of Pain*, pg.21

[219] *Miracles*, ch.5

[220] Bruce R. McConkie, *Mormon Doctrine*, pg.156 CONSCIENCE

[221] Lewis, C.S. *Mere Christianity*. Collier Books. Macmillan Publishing Company, 1952. pg.6

[222] *Teachings of Ezra Taft Benson*, (God, Family, Country, p.156.) pg.355

[223] *Teachings of Ezra Taft Benson*, pg.601

[224] Teachings of Ezra Taft Benson, pg.456 ("Your Charge: To Increase in Wisdom and Favor with God and Man," *New Era* 9 [September 1979]: 40.)

[225] Lewis, C.S. *Mere Christianity*. Collier Books. Macmillan Publishing Company, 1952. pg.7

[226] Bruce R. McConkie, Mormon Doctrine, pg.810 TRUTH

[227] Lewis, C.S. *Mere Christianity*. Collier Books. Macmillan Publishing Company, 1952. pg.10

[228] Bruce R. McConkie, Mormon Doctrine, pg.811 TRUTH

[229] Lewis, C.S. *Mere Christianity*. Collier Books. Macmillan Publishing Company, 1952. pg.11

[230] *The Abolition of Man*, ch.2

[231] Lewis, C.S. *Mere Christianity*. Collier Books. Macmillan Publishing Company, 1952. pg.56

[232] Lewis, C.S. *The Problem of Pain*. New York: The Macmillan Company, 1962. pg.94

[233] Alma 42:25

[234] *History of the Church*, Vol.3, Introduction, pg.41

[235] D&C 76:38

[236] *Teachings of Ezra Taft Benson*, pg.617

[237] David O. McKay, *Gospel Ideals*, pg.349

[238] *Teachings of Ezra Taft Benson*, pg.188

[239] *Teachings of Ezra Taft Benson*, ("The Light of Christmas," Christmas Lighting Ceremony, Temple Square, Salt Lake City, Utah, 26 November 1982.) pg.359

[240] Lewis, C.S. *The Problem of Pain*. New York: The Macmillan Company, 1962. pg.103-4

[241] *Teachings of Ezra Taft Benson*, ("New Year 1961," Washington D.C. Ward, 31 December 1960.) pg.339

[242] Spencer W. Kimball, *The Miracle of Forgiveness*, pg.259

[243] Lewis, C.S. *Mere Christianity*. Collier Books. Macmillan Publishing Company, 1952. pg.39

[244] Teachings of Ezra Taft Benson, pg.79

[245] Lewis, C.S. *Mere Christianity*. Collier Books. Macmillan Publishing Company, 1952. pg.58

[246] Ibid. pg.63

[247] Mark E. Petersen, *The Way to Peace*, pg.25

[248] *Letters of C.S. Lewis* (17 July 1953)

[249] *Mere Christianity*, bk 2, ch.3

[250] *Man or Rabbit*

[251] Unpublished letter (August 1, 1953)

[252] Lewis, C.S. *Mere Christianity*. Collier Books. Macmillan Publishing Company, 1952. pg.137

253 Bruce R. McConkie, *Mormon Doctrine*, pg.192 DESTRUCTION OF THE SOUL

254 Lewis, C.S. *Mere Christianity*. Collier Books. Macmillan Publishing Company, 1952. pg.65-6

255 *Discourses of Brigham Young*, pg.198

256 Bruce R. McConkie, *The Promised Messiah*, pg.553

257 Lewis, C.S. *Mere Christianity*. Collier Books. Macmillan Publishing Company, 1952. pg.66

258 Bruce R. McConkie, *Mormon Doctrine*, pg.152 COMMUNISM

259 Lewis, C.S. *The Problem of Pain*. New York: The Macmillan Company, 1962. pg.91

260 Neal A. Maxwell, *Men and Women of Christ*, pg.8

261 Ibid. pg.2

262 Ibid. pg.8-9

263 Ibid. pg.11

264 Lewis, C.S. *The Problem of Pain*. New York: The Macmillan Company, 1962. pg.92

265 Ibid. pg.106-7

266 Lewis, C.S. *Mere Christianity*. Collier Books. Macmillan Publishing Company, 1952. pg.44-45

267 Ibid. pg.53

268 Neal A. Maxwell, *We Talk of Christ*, Pg129-30

269 Lewis, C.S. *Mere Christianity*. Collier Books. Macmillan Publishing Company, 1952. pg.150

270 Neal A. Maxwell, *That My Family Should Partake*, pg.41

271 Joseph Fielding Smith, *Gospel Doctrine*, pg.440

272 Lewis, C.S. *Mere Christianity*. Collier Books. Macmillan Publishing Company, 1952. pg.154-5

273 Neal A. Maxwell, *All These Things Shall Give Thee Experience*, pg.2

274 Neal A. Maxwell, *Not My Will, But Thine*, pg.9

275 Lewis, C.S. *Mere Christianity*. Collier Books. Macmillan Publishing Company, 1952. pg.175

276 Ibid.

277 An *Experiment in Criticism, Epilogue*

278 Lewis, C.S. *Mere Christianity*. Collier Books. Macmillan Publishing Company, 1952. pg.167

279 Ibid. pg.20

280 Ibid. pg.23

281 Harold B. Lee, Conference Report, April 1963, p.88

282 *Collected Works of Hugh Nibley*, Vol.3, ch.15, pg.132-133

283 Lewis, C.S. *Mere Christianity*. Collier Books. Macmillan Publishing Company, 1952. pg.129

284 Ibid. pg.32-3

285 Neal A. Maxwell, *All These Things Shall Give Thee Experience*, pg.3-4

286 Lewis, C.S. *Mere Christianity*. Collier Books. Macmillan Publishing Company, 1952. pg.5

287 'A Christian Reply to Professor Price' (Phoenix Quarterly, Autumn 1946)

288 *Lectures on Faith*, Lecture 6, pg.58

289 *Letters to Malcolm*, ch.14

290 Lewis, C.S. *Mere Christianity*. Collier Books. Macmillan Publishing Company, 1952. pg.21

291 *Collected Works of Hugh Nibley*, Vol.3, ch.15, pg.129

292 Lewis, C.S. *The Problem of Pain*. New York: The Macmillan Company, 1962. pg.26

293 Ibid. pg.40

294 2 Nephi 2:11

295 D&C 128:24

296 Lewis, C.S. *The Problem of Pain*. New York: The Macmillan Company, 1962. pg.42-43

297 Ibid. pg.44

298 Moses 4:14

[299] Lewis, C.S. *The Problem of Pain*. New York: The Macmillan Company, 1962. pg.93
[300] Ibid. pg.97
[301] Spencer W. Kimball, *The Miracle of Forgiveness*, pg.48
[302] Lewis, C.S. *The Problem of Pain*. New York: The Macmillan Company, 1962. pg.146-7
[303] James E. Talmage, *Jesus the Christ*, ch.3, pg.29 Also see James E. Talmage, *The Great Apostasy*, pg.19-20
[304] Bruce R. McConkie, *Mormon Doctrine*, pg.588 PREDESTINATION
[305] Lewis, C.S. *The Screwtape Letters*. Collier Books — Macmillan Publishing Company. NEW YORK, 1961. pg.128
[306] Lewis, C.S. *The Screwtape Letters*. Collier Books — Macmillan Publishing Company. NEW YORK, 1961. pg.170
[307] Conference Report, April 1963, pg.69
[308] Alma 36:20
[309] *The Teachings of Spencer W. Kimball*, pg.40
[310] *Transposition and Other Addresses*
[311] D&C 63:66
[312] Lewis, C.S. *Mere Christianity*. Collier Books. Macmillan Publishing Company, 1952. pg.23-4
[313] Marion D. Hanks, Conference Report, October 1967, pg.59
[314] Lewis, C.S. *Mere Christianity*. Collier Books. Macmillan Publishing Company, 1952. pg.113
[315] Mosiah 4:11
[316] Lewis, C.S. *Mere Christianity*. Collier Books. Macmillan Publishing Company, 1952. pg.110
[317] Lewis, C.S. *The Problem of Pain*. New York: The Macmillan Company, 1962. pg.80
[318] Neal A. Maxwell, *Men and Women of Christ*, pg.14
[319] Gibbs, Nancy. "The Message of Miracles." *TIME*. April 10, 1995.
[320] Lewis, C.S. *The Problem of Pain*. New York: The Macmillan Company, 1962. pg.23-4
[321] Teachings of Ezra Taft Benson, pg.104
[322] Joseph Smith History, pg.59 (Scriptures)
[323] Lewis, C.S. *Mere Christianity*. Collier Books. Macmillan Publishing Company, 1952. pg.41
[324] Joseph Fielding Smith Jr., *Doctrines of Salvation*, Vol.1, pg.315
[325] *Mere Christianity*, bk 2, ch.3
[326] *Miracles*, ch.11
[327] Teachings of Ezra Taft Benson, pg.9 ("Easter 1966 — A Quest for the True Jesus," *Newsweek*, April 11, 1966, p.72)
[328] *Teachings of Ezra Taft Benson*, pg.127
[329] 'What Are We to Make of Jesus Christ?' *Asking Them Questions*
[330] Lewis, C.S. *Mere Christianity*. Collier Books. Macmillan Publishing Company, 1952. pg.121
[331] *The World's Last Night*, ch.7
[332] N. Eldon Tanner, Conference Report, October 1966, pg.48
[333] Matthew 16:16